MY TURN AT BAT
The Sad Saga of the Montreal Expos

By Claude Brochu

Daniel Poulin and Mario Bolduc

Translated by
Stephanie Myles

ECW PRESS

Copyright © ECW PRESS, 2002

Published by ECW PRESS
2120 Queen Street East, Suite 200, Toronto, Ontario, Canada M4E 1E2

NATIONAL LIBRARY OF CANADA CATALOGUING IN PUBLICATION DATA

Brochu, Claude
My turn at bat: the sad saga of the Montreal Expos

Translation of: La saga des Expos.
ISBN 1-55022-512-X

1. Montreal Expos (Baseball team)—History.
2. Baseball—Quebec (Province)—Montreal—History.
I. Poulin, Daniel, 1944- II. Bolduc, Mario III. Myles, Stephanie IV. Title.
V. Title: The sad saga of the Montreal Expos.

GV875.M6B7513 2002   796.357'64'0971428   C2001-904291-4

Cover photo: Bernard Préfontaine
Acquisition Editor: Robert Lecker
Editor: Dallas Harrison
Cover design: Guylaine Régimbald—Solo Design
Text design and typesetting: Yolande Martel
Production: Heather Bean
Printing: Transcontinental

This book is set in Janson and Trade Gothic

The publication of *My Turn at Bat* has been generously supported by the Canada Council, the Ontario Arts Council, and the Government of Canada through the Book Industry Development Program. Canadä

DISTRIBUTION

CANADA: General Distribution Services, 325 Humber College Blvd., Toronto, ON M9W 7C3

UNITED STATES: Independent Publishers Group, 814 North Franklin Street, Chicago, Illinois 60610

EUROPE: Turnaround Publisher Services, Unit 3, Olympia Trading Estate, Coburg Road, Wood Green, London N22 6T2

AUSTRALIA AND NEW ZEALAND: Wakefield Press, 17 Rundle Street (Box 2066), Kent Town, South Australia 5071

PRINTED AND BOUND IN CANADA

ECW PRESS
ecwpress.com

To my spouse, Michelle,
for her love and support

Table of Contents

Foreword

In 1969, for the first time in the history of Major League Baseball, a team from outside the United States embarked on its regular season. The birth of the Expos allowed Montreal to become part of "the big leagues," a unique privilege. Thirty-three years later, this fantastic experience is ending. Montreal will soon lose its baseball team.

Why? What could possibly have happened to get to this point? All the fans, all those who worked with and for the team, all Quebecers—all Canadians, really—deserve to know the real reasons for this failure.

From the start, the team's existence was never easy. "The Expos against the world" might well have been the ball club's motto in those early days. Both John McHale, my predecessor as president, and I quickly realized the Expos were waging a constant battle for survival.

Discussions with the Quebec health-insurance board (RAMQ) and the Olympic Installations Board (OIB), dealings with the various levels of government, the negotiation of radio and television broadcasting rights, the revenue-sharing program, the often-negative attitude of the media, a lukewarm corporate community, and, of course, the weakness of the Canadian dollar all joined forces in threatening the very existence of the franchise.

Yet, against all odds, the Expos built a solid organization that quickly became a model for Major League Baseball. The team itself became a leader among franchises operating in markets considered marginal.

The numerous responsibilities entrusted to me allowed me to increase the Expos' influence in the baseball industry. In 1995, I became the first Canadian elected to Major League Baseball's Executive Council, and following that I joined the National League's Executive Committee. I also chaired the Operations Committee, which oversees all of baseball's minor-league activities (farm teams, international development leagues, as well as scouting, among other areas). I was also on the Board of Directors of Baseball Enterprises, whose principal mandate is to generate the industry's revenues.

Unfortunately, in 1998, "The Expos against the world" became "Expos versus Expos." The members of the consortium that now owned the team began tearing each other to pieces—sometimes even publicly. These internecine power struggles nipped the downtown Montreal stadium project in the bud. As the leader of this ambitious project, which could have ensured the presence of the Expos in Montreal for years to come, I was to be eliminated.

Much has been said and written about the never-ending saga of the Expos—a few truths but many more falsehoods. The subject has stirred up a lot of passion.

I found myself in the middle of this raging storm from the very beginning. For a long time, I thought reason and common sense would prevail. But when I realized the project had no hope of succeeding, I chose to bow out. To this day, I still believe building the stadium was the right thing to do.

Subsequent events have only confirmed my fears. Many have admitted that I was right, that I should have been listened to at the time. "You must be having the last laugh," I've been told a few times. Others have said, "They put so much of the blame on you. Something is definitely 'not right' about this whole story. . . ."

To a good number of my detractors, money was the sole motivation for my actions and eventual departure. That is false, of course, as this book will demonstrate.

I'm not attempting to defend myself; rather, I'm trying to explain what really happened. I want to try to answer the question everyone is asking. How could Jeffrey Loria have so easily duped the elite of the Quebec business world? In my opinion, the problems didn't appear with the arrival of the new majority partner. They began to appear a lot earlier than that.

I consciously and deliberately chose to issue no formal or public comment after my departure from the Expos. It wasn't that I didn't want to, believe me—particularly after I was accused of weaving a Machiavellian plot to spirit the club out of Montreal! Exactly the opposite was true. Nothing was dearer to my heart than the success of a ball club to which I'd dedicated 13 years of my life. The time has come to present a serious, comprehensive analysis of the final years of the Expos, one born of my inside knowledge of the subject.

This book outlines the numerous obstacles and complex difficulties faced by professional sports teams operating in small markets. It deals with the back-door politics of the Expos' limited partnership. And it attempts to explain why the new downtown stadium project ended in failure. Above all, it tells a story that could have had—no, should have had—a happy ending. If only people had cared enough to try. . . .

Preface

When my friend Claude Brochu asked me to write a preface for his book on the saga of the Montreal Expos, I found myself torn. On the one hand, I had success with the Expos thanks to a majority partner who was the real boss, a professional management team, and ballplayers who were well paid but, above all, loved to play the game. On the other hand, this book was going to criticize people whom I also considered friends.

I agreed to do it because Claude continued to be my friend—even after I told him that I didn't believe in the new stadium project and that baseball and hockey were doomed unless the sports established player salary caps and learned to live within their means. You don't need a degree in economics to understand that paying players in U.S. dollars, while a team's revenues are in Canadian dollars, can be nothing but ruinously expensive.

This book helped me to understand the end of the 1970s (1977–80), when I was the Expos' vice president of marketing and public affairs, was one of the finest periods in the franchise's history as much on the field as in the front office. And it confirmed what I have always believed: if it is good to get a consensus, it is essential that there be a single pilot at the controls. It proved a professional ball club must be the property of one person who can live with his or her decisions. This book made me see that too much goodwill is the same as not enough and that the glare of the spotlight can be blinding. And that, as long as man exists, so will his weaknesses.

Readers will draw their own conclusions. For my part, I ask myself how so many rich, competent, and dedicated men could have let this happen.

Claude had a plan to minimize his shareholders' losses while awaiting a long-term solution, and to that end he had a plan to provide Montreal with a new downtown stadium that could ensure the Expos' survival. Influenced by ever-impatient armchair managers eager to pass judgement without knowing all the facts, the shareholders and other captains of industry who appeared on the scene didn't believe in him. And they all wanted to take the controls at once. Ultimately, they were pitifully outmanoeuvred by the newcomer whom they'd chosen—with the disastrous results of which we are all aware. In this saga, they lost far more than their respective investments.

This book is full of lessons to be learned. Happy reading.

Introduction

I first met Claude Brochu in the spring of 1989. I was working for Radio-Canada in Toronto, and CBLFT (now defunct) was preparing to broadcast the first Toronto Blue Jays game at the brand-new SkyDome. I was to do the play-by-play, with Claude Raymond providing the colour commentary.

To secure Raymond's services, we first had to get permission from his boss, since the former star pitcher was an Expos' employee. I introduced myself to Brochu during a game at Olympic Stadium. I asked him directly if he'd allow Raymond to work the game between the Blue Jays and the Milwaukee Brewers in Toronto. His answer was as brief as it was spontaneous, with a little humour thrown in for good measure. "Gladly, but don't make a habit of it," he said. Right then I liked the man.

In 1995, I moved to Montreal, where I covered events on the regional scene on a freelance basis for Radio-Canada. After attending an Expos press conference where we began to sense a major problem brewing within the organization, sports department head Yvon Vadnais asked me to follow the story closely. I dove into what would become an endless, obscure saga riddled with troubling, difficult-to-analyse contradictions.

I had a front-row seat for the slow disintegration of this organization, orchestrated by a group of businessmen considered to be the *crème de la crème* of the group often identified as "Quebec Inc." Throughout the numerous and fascinating twists and turns that marked the three years of my coverage of the story, one constant appeared: the lack of clarity and openness from just about everyone involved—the partners themselves and the Major League Baseball executives entrenched in their legendary silence.

Another reality quickly came to light: the relentless determination of just about everyone involved to point the finger at one man, one lone man, as being responsible for everything that ailed the Expos. When my bosses asked me why I was waiting so long to add my voice to those of colleagues who'd appointed themselves both judge and jury on Brochu, I answered that I simply wanted proof he was as dishonest and malicious as they claimed. I'm still waiting for that proof.

The February 1999 press conference during which the partners called on Brochu to be a good citizen and bow out was the turning point for me. How could mature and intelligent men resort to such tactics, with such impunity, to achieve their ends? And how could reporters and columnists fall for this message of hate and propagate it without restraint or judgement? All of that remains a mystery to me.

Because I never pilloried Brochu in my reporting, I was often accused of being in cahoots with him. For the record, never during these critical years did he try, directly or indirectly, to communicate with me. My only contact with the Expos' organization was made through regular channels, through Johanne Héroux, vice president of communications, or the team's media-relations staff—hardly well informed themselves, I might add.

One man, however, did play a major role in my research during this long saga. And he appeared via an unusual combination of circumstances. One Friday afternoon, moments before the early-evening sportscast, Radio-Canada assistant news editor Mychel St-Louis brought me a confidential document. It was a letter signed by Major League Baseball commissioner Bud Selig and addressed to Claude Brochu and Jacques Ménard, a letter that sharply reprimanded Ménard and asked him to hold his tongue. There was no doubt it was a blockbuster document. We decided to lead our late-night sportscast with it and gave it to *La Presse*, which made it a line story in its Saturday edition. At that point, I didn't know the source of this leak and didn't dare ask.

Finally, I learned from my colleague Philippe Schnobb—who covered the Expos' story for Radio-Canada—that the informer was Richard Le Lay, the *éminence grise* of Brochu. I contacted him, and we quickly developed a special relationship marked by mutual respect. He was a valuable help to me as the saga unfolded, without ever trying to influence my judgement.

Another incident worth mentioning: a few days after the revelation of the commissioner's letter, I received a call from Ménard, who, in a very annoyed tone of voice, warned me about "people who had their own agenda." This attempt at intimidation from the Expos' chairman was part of a most unseemly strategy to influence—no, control—the information communicated to the public. After consulting my supervisor, I decided to react in writing (see appendix, letter dated February 17, 1999, page 235).

My association with Radio-Canada ended in 1999. I found myself with a lot of free time on my hands. During a social encounter with Le Lay and Brochu, I said, jokingly, that it would be fun to write a book about the Expos' saga. Imagine my astonishment to hear Brochu respond, "Why don't we do it together, Daniel?" That was how the book project, which sees the light of day as the Expos say good-bye, was born.

The past number of months have allowed me to know a warm and remarkable man. In my mind, there is no doubt Claude Brochu is a man of both integrity and sincerity. Certainly, he has made mistakes; who hasn't? But at the end of the day, he can walk with his head held high. His story is worth reading; it sheds light on a period of our collective lives as Quebecers that may not be our shining hour but nevertheless reveals much about our unique nature. We can only hope it serves as a lesson for future generations.

I am firmly convinced the eventual departure of the Expos won't be the end of the world for Montreal. The enviable reputation of our superb city rests on values far deeper than the success of a professional sports team made up of athletes, foreigners all, who'd much rather be elsewhere. Their wish will soon be granted; may they be the better for it.

CHAPTER 1

Charles Bronfman's Decision

The lobby of Nashville's Opryland Hotel was a nonstop, colourful whirlwind of activity. Men and women from across America, many of them in blue jeans, cowboy boots on their feet. A casual atmosphere, even if the assets these individuals represented added up to hundreds of millions of dollars.

Their common passion? Baseball.

Major League Baseball owners arrived at the Opryland Hotel with their entire staffs: general managers, field managers, scouts, coaches, trainers. . . . All had one goal: to take advantage of this week in Nashville to start or continue trade talks, close deals, and improve their teams not only for the upcoming season but also for the longer term.

Over the course of the previous season, each club's scouts evaluated every player in the major and minor leagues and determined the strengths and weaknesses of the opposing teams. They endeavoured to find young, talented, but still-unknown players. Their efforts covered more than 600 major-league players and several thousand minor leaguers.

No surprise, then, the lobby on that December day resembled a public market—a market where the future of each of the 26 major-league teams (in 1989) was being shaped.

The general managers run the show at the winter meetings, sending their people to put out feelers with the other teams. When talks appear to be heading somewhere, once they get past the bluffing stage and the empty promises, representatives from both clubs find themselves in one or the other team's suite. There trades take shape, are refined, get complicated. The general managers and their advisors examine the offers, counter them, all based on the evaluation work that took place during the just-completed season.

Finally, in the wee hours, when an agreement is reached, the media are convened. All week long, reporters from across the United States and Canada have had their collective ear to the ground for the latest news, the juiciest rumours, which they report back to those reading their hometown newspapers and watching the major television networks. In the press conferences, some of those rumours become realities.

At the end of the winter meetings, the National and American Leagues can be transformed. When the experts head home for the holidays, many are convinced they've improved their teams. But they will have to wait for the upcoming season to find out if the trades and agreements concluded that week will bear fruit. Wait to find out if the Christmas presents they gave to themselves truly are gifts.

These weren't my first winter meetings. But the 1989 edition in Nashville will forever remain etched in my memory. I'd been president of the Montreal Expos since 1986. I was the big boss— after Charles Bronfman, obviously, the majority owner of the ball club.

Born in Quebec City, the son of a military man, I'd always been adaptable to very different universes. During my elementary and high school years, I changed schools nine times—and it certainly wasn't because of my grades. Quite the opposite; my father's career took my family to several countries. As a result, I spent my childhood all over Canada and in Europe.

At first, after earning a bachelor's degree in history at the University of Ottawa, I wanted to follow in my father's army footsteps. But after a few years as an officer in the Royal 22nd Regiment, I realized I wasn't cut out for military life. I changed directions again. I went to McMaster University in Hamilton, where I earned my MBA.

I'd found my path: business—more specifically, marketing. I cut my teeth at Avon and Cosmair. Then I went to Seagrams, where I quickly climbed the ladder to become executive vice president of marketing for Canada.

But my passion was baseball. As a child, I played on local clubs. Later I closely followed the creation of the Montreal Expos. I attended the team's games, first at Jarry Park, then at Olympic Stadium. While at Seagrams, I often devoted my vacations to base-ball. At my own expense, I travelled to the Expos' spring-training camp in West Palm Beach, Florida.

By 1986, I was running the ball club.

I adored the winter meetings. I loved rubbing shoulders with the owners of the other clubs; being part of this select group of businesspeople was both fascinating and amusing. It takes a certain amount of detachment to be able to move about a group made up of sometimes-megalomaniacal multimillionaires.

Happily, my boss, Charles Bronfman, even though he was wealthier than any of the other owners, had nothing of the arro-gance and self-importance some of them displayed. At the Opryland Hotel, Bronfman occupied a relatively modest room by their stan-dards. The Expos' owner didn't always accompany me to the winter meetings. But that year he was there.

One night he summoned me to his room. He wanted to talk to me. In a few minutes, we'd join our staff for dinner. He poured me a Chivas Regal; he himself sipped a Seagrams vo, naturally.

Bronfman and I had known each other for several years. Since my arrival at Seagrams, we'd gotten along well—and not just dur-ing business hours. On the tennis courts, particularly. It wasn't rare, on weekends, to find us playing doubles together.

But baseball—Bronfman's great passion—helped to make us closer. In May 1968, thanks to the efforts of Mayor Jean Drapeau and Executive Committee vice president Gerry Snyder, Montreal was awarded a Major League Baseball franchise, along with San Diego. In August of that year, Bronfman handed a cheque for $1 million to National League president Warren Giles, the first instalment of the $10 million fee required by the league. John McHale was named president of the team.

When McHale decided to retire in 1986, Bronfman asked me, after a tennis game, to suggest replacements. Even though McHale had done an excellent job heading up the Expos, Bronfman wanted the new president to better understand, and better attract, the francophone public. The ideal candidate should therefore be francophone and bilingual, know the game, and demonstrate leadership. Most of all, he needed to have Bronfman's complete trust. I suggested some names, but Bronfman wasn't convinced.

Several weeks later—once again on the tennis court—we had a breakthrough. Bronfman had often told his wife, Andrea, how difficult it was to find a replacement for McHale. Finally, she'd replied, "The ideal candidate? You play tennis with him! No need to look any further. . . ." Her thoughts on the subject had incited Bronfman to take a closer look at his tennis partner. He realized his wife was right; I'd make a good president. We knew each other well, respected each other. I loved baseball and had proven my leadership ability at Seagrams.

When Bronfman officially offered me the job, I was stunned. At that point, my career path was already mapped out. I liked my job, my responsibilities. I saw myself, over the years, continuing to rise through the company's ranks. I'd never imagined Bronfman would call on me to run the Expos.

After the initial shock wore off, I thought over the proposal. Bronfman's confidence in me pleased me greatly, but the pressure was tremendous. Yet what sports fan hasn't dreamed of running a professional team? It was an incredible opportunity I had no intention of passing up. I was 41 years old. I decided to dive right in.

Three years later, in Bronfman's room at the Opryland Hotel, I could assess the road travelled since October 1, 1986. The three years as president had been stimulating for me but frustrating on several levels.

Since 1983, when the Expos attracted more than 2,320,000 fans, annual attendance had always been below 2,000,000. In 1989, only

1,783,533 fans went through the Olympic Stadium turnstiles. And there was no indication the situation would improve in the coming years.

Bronfman was an Expos *fan*, the most avid of them all. He rarely missed a home game; he often stayed up until the wee hours listening to the broadcasts from the West Coast.

Over the past few seasons, when Bronfman attended a game, the first question he'd ask me was this: "How many are there tonight?"

And I'd answer 10,000, 15,000, 25,000. . . . Since the beginning of the 1980s, crowds in excess of 30,000 had become increasingly rare.

Bronfman would shake his head, discouraged. "But why don't they come? What do we have to do?"

Field a winning team was the answer from the media and the armchair managers.

In 1989, Expos' management took that advice to heart and acquired lefthander Mark Langston from the Seattle Mariners, following the recommendation of general manager Dave Dombrowski. On May 28, in his first start in an Expos uniform, Langston impressed everyone. Here, finally, was the pitcher we'd long been waiting for! The one who'd lead the Expos to a championship.

As expected, the club slowly rose in the standings. In fourth place in May, two games behind the leaders, the Expos found themselves atop the division a month later. And at the all-star break. They remained there until the beginning of August.

That's when Langston crumbled, at Shea Stadium in New York against the Mets. Unable to muster up a performance he considered worthy of his talent, he elected to take himself out of a game the Expos were leading 2-1. Tim Burke replaced him, but the bullpen couldn't hold the lead. The Expos lost 3-2.

They were swept by the Mets and fell out of the division lead. Another sweep followed in another three-game series, this one against the Chicago Cubs.

After Langston's "performance," team morale dropped through the floor. Bronfman and I both knew the team wouldn't recover. The Expos finished the season in fourth place.

To get Langston, we had to give up good players—among them, Randy Johnson. Today Johnson is one of the premier pitchers in the game, one every manager dreams of having on his team. Pitchers Brian Holman and Gene Harris were also part of the trade. Three players, then, far too much, according to Bronfman, who'd have preferred to give up only two pitchers to the Mariners.

It was a bad deal, one that would greatly affect Bronfman, Dombrowski, and me. Witnessing the decline of the ball club in the ensuing weeks was trying for us, especially after we'd paid such a heavy price for the chance to participate in a World Series.

But when I met with Bronfman in his Nashville hotel room, the end-of-summer depression was already a thing of the past. I was ready to roll up my sleeves and get back to work. Bronfman, however, wasn't nearly as enthusiastic. He turned to me and said, "Claude, I want to sell the ball club. . . ."

"I can't believe it," I replied.

"I don't have the strength to fight anymore. I'm not having fun. I'm tired. . . ."

I couldn't believe what I was hearing. I was certain my boss would get over the difficult season we'd just lived through. One shouldn't rush things, base such a decision purely on the emotion of the moment.

But the Expos' owner was determined. I clearly saw I wouldn't be able to change his mind. For Bronfman, the Expos weren't just a business; they were a true passion. There's no doubt the $10 million he invested in 1968 would have brought a better return elsewhere. The decision to get involved in this adventure was, above all, an emotional one. So was the decision to get out of it.

The poor results of the previous season weren't the only factor for Bronfman. Baseball had always been an integral part of his life. He knew it as a sport, of course, but also as a business. He counted several owners among his close friends. After 21 years of heading up the Expos, he now was one of the elder statesmen in the game.

But over the years, the management of professional baseball had changed. Prestigious owners such as Walter O'Malley, Horace

Stoneham, Philip Wrigley, Bob Carpenter, and John Galbraith—true baseball lovers—had slowly but surely been replaced by corporations interested more in a return on their investment than in the game itself. It was now a business like any other.

And then there were the players, whose behaviour toward the owners was reprehensible at times. Everyone, it seemed, was concerned only with personal financial interests, the players as much as anyone else.

Bronfman was uncomfortable in that environment. The club's collapse the previous year, his inability to attract fans, the working climate, all had visibly exhausted him.

"Sell?" I asked. "But to whom?"

"I don't know, but I want you to handle it. I want you to find buyers. . . ."

"It would be more normal if it were you. . . ."

"I don't see who has the means, in Quebec, to acquire the team."

"In my opinion, I think you could get $75 million," I said.

"Really?" Bronfman replied, surprised. "I thought $50 million would be more realistic. . . ."

Regardless of the price, we were convinced buyers would hardly be beating down the door. I knew Bronfman had already tried to convince Paul Desmarais of Power Corporation to become his partner in the Expos. But Desmarais had refused.

"What if you called upon the services of a financial institution to make sure the transaction is handled properly?" Bronfman then suggested.

I thought it was an excellent idea. But there was something else to take care of first: my future with the organization. I could either leave once my work was done or stay with the team. I didn't hesitate. Bronfman was looking back, but I was thinking of the future. For more than 20 years, the team had been part of the lives of Quebecers, of Montrealers in particular. Bronfman's departure was the perfect opportunity for francophone Quebecers to get more involved with the organization. I wanted to be part of the group that would make it happen.

Bronfman was right: other than Power Corporation, no Quebec company by itself could afford to take over. But a consortium of Quebec and Canadian companies might be able to manage it. We had to find an original formula, a working framework that would ensure the development of the team while still respecting the requirements set out by Major League Baseball.

That night at dinner, sitting with my management team, my mind was elsewhere. I was aware Bronfman's departure would mean the end of an era, the end of a management style. And I knew only too well the mandate entrusted to me wasn't a simple one. If I couldn't find buyers within the prescribed time frame, Bronfman would have no other alternative but to offer the club to American interests who would probably want to move it to a U.S. city. I absolutely had to succeed, or it would be the end of baseball in Montreal.

I made it a personal challenge. Those in business are often portrayed as cold, emotionless people who make decisions based only on the eventual possibility of making a lot of money. Soap, cars, whatever—as long as it sells. But, at least for me, that wasn't it at all. Of course, I knew that the team could be profitable and that I could come out a winner, but that financial aspect was secondary. What fascinated me, what motivated me, was to keep the Expos in Montreal, in the hands of Quebecers—one of those Quebecers being me.

CHAPTER 2

The First Steps

The sale of a professional baseball club is hardly a typical financial transaction. Even though Charles Bronfman owned the Expos, he couldn't divest himself of the club however he thought best. The deal first had to be submitted to Major League Baseball's Ownership Committee, which would ensure it conformed to industry norms. Of course, the committee takes into account the stability and solvency of the new owner. But every detail of the sale is also carefully examined. If any aspect or condition of the transaction doesn't meet with the committee's approval, modifications must be made.

In other words, the process of selling a team is closely supervised by Major League Baseball executives, who refuse to cave in to outside pressures. The buyer's eagerness to close a deal with a crafty seller has no impact whatsoever on their decision.

As soon as he was advised of Bronfman's decision, Jerry Reinsdorf, owner of the Chicago White Sox and chairman of the Ownership Committee, explained his conditions. A fat cigar in his mouth, extremely sure of himself, Reinsdorf was the embodiment of the image most people have of a Major League Baseball executive. And he was an executive who exercised obvious influence over the other owners.

Reinsdorf agreed with Bronfman: the Expos had to stay in Montreal. He also hoped that Canadian investors would purchase the team or that an appeal would be made to an American investor ready to set up shop in Montreal. If we couldn't succeed in that endeavour, the participation of an American investor who didn't live in Canada was possible—on the condition, of course, that the club remain in Montreal. If none of these solutions was feasible, only then could the club be sold to American interests and transferred to another city.

Once Reinsdorf and his committee approved the transaction, it would then be submitted to the National and American League owners, who'd have to ratify it. At that moment, and not before, the Expos' change of ownership could be confirmed.

Back in Montreal, in my office at Olympic Stadium, I went to work. When Bronfman suggested I call on a financial institution or a brokerage firm, he was thinking chiefly of major companies such as Coopers & Lybrand or Price Waterhouse. I proposed instead to entrust the mandate to a company that, as I saw it, was closer to the financial interests in Quebec. A company that had closer ties to large francophone companies.

I settled on Burns Fry, a firm run by Jacques Ménard, which specialized in the financing, merger, and acquisition of companies. A native of Chicoutimi, the 43-year-old Ménard was one of the most dynamic brokers in the securities industry, in which he'd worked since 1970. President of the Montreal Chamber of Commerce, Ménard was exactly the type of partner I was searching for: a francophone, from the new wave of Quebec business, whose contacts in Quebec would facilitate the search for investors.

We got acquainted at Bocca D'Oro, a downtown Italian restaurant. Jean Lajoie, a Burns Fry associate and Ménard's principal advisor, was also present. From the start, the three of us got along marvellously. The project was exciting; Ménard and his team immediately agreed to participate. For Burns Fry, the Expos' name and reputation made it a jewel in the crown of Quebec's business world. And, of course, the sales commission was hardly insignificant. Jean Elie, head of government relations for Burns Fry, and Luigi Fraquelli would join the team later.

Bronfman approved the selection of Burns Fry. He also believed associating a Quebec firm with the sales team was an excellent idea.

The members of the Expos' Board of Directors—Hugh Hallward and Lorne Webster (Bronfman's two minority partners), Senator E. Leo Kolber, Arnie Ludwick, and John McHale—also approved the selection of Ménard as financial consultant.

It was now up to Bronfman to name the sales team that would negotiate with Ménard, the others, and me. Two men were chosen: Robert Vineberg of the firm Phillips & Vineberg, the Bronfman family's longtime legal advisors, and Robert Rabinovitch, today president of the Canadian Boadcasting Corporation (CBC) but then the top executive at Claridge, the investment firm owned by Bronfman and his immediate family.

The first step was the preparation by the Burns Fry team and Expos' management of a confidential information memorandum, a prospectus that explained the terms of the acquisition, stated the present value and the future value of the team, and outlined the revenue possibilities of such a company. A confidential document, to be sure; there hadn't yet been an official announcement the team was for sale. When the time came, this document would be distributed to Quebec companies thought to have an interest in investing in the Expos.

But before offering the team to potential investors, a major issue had to be determined: the positions of the governments.

In the United States, governments play no role in the sale of a professional baseball team. Public bodies, even at the municipal level, never invest in the ownership of a team. In Canada, particularly in Quebec, the situation is different. In the United States, the wealth is often long-standing and in the hands of individuals and private companies, while in Quebec—with a few exceptions—wealth is recent and institutional.

In this context, Ménard and I had no choice. The various levels of government had to be involved in the sale of the Expos but in such a way as not to upset Major League Baseball.

Happily, the Expos had a powerful ally in Quebec City: Robert Bourassa. The premier was a baseball fan: he watched many games on television, with his radio tuned in to Rodger Brulotte's radio broadcast, and he considered that for society sport was as important as culture. One thing was certain: Bourassa didn't want the Expos to leave Quebec. An economist by trade, he also judged the presence of a professional baseball team in Montreal a good thing from an economic point of view.

Bourassa carefully planned his involvement regarding the purchase of the team. He was aware Quebecers would never approve of any direct government aid. So he carefully suggested we go through intermediaries such as the Olympic Installations Board (OIB), which oversees Olympic Stadium for the government, and—with the approval of his minister of finance—the Société de développement industriel (SDI), a provincial government investment company.

Bourassa wanted to twin his involvement with that of the City of Montreal. "If Montreal gets involved with the Expos, the provincial government will do the same," he said. The city could use the same argument. Bourassa knew that, whatever gesture his government made, it would be a precedent that could eventually apply to the National Hockey League Quebec Nordiques—whose future was already worrisome. (Had Bourassa lived, I'm certain he'd have found a way to save the Nordiques.)

OIB president Pierre Bibeau also played a crucial role in the survival of the Expos. Contrary to some of his OIB colleagues, Bibeau believed in Olympic Stadium as a sports venue. He sensitized Louise Harel, MNA for the Maisonneuve riding in which the stadium was located, to the situation and received her support for Bourassa's proposal. Harel did the same with opposition leader Jacques Parizeau. The position of the Parti Québécois was identical to that of the government. Direct aid was out of the question, but it agreed with the premier's approach.

The plan to help out the Expos financially, whether directly or indirectly, obviously didn't create unanimity within the government. At cabinet meetings, several ministers expressed their disagreement—notably Minister of Finance Daniel Johnson. But since the premier himself had originated the project, none of his ministers dared be too vocal. The Expos could therefore count on solid support from the Quebec government.

But Bourassa went even further. One afternoon he invited Ménard, Elie, and me to his residence on Maplewood Avenue in Outremont. During that meeting, he proposed this: "I'll call a few business leaders on your behalf to encourage them to get involved in the acquisition of the Expos," he said.

"And the government will participate in what way?" I asked.

"Through the sdi, probably. A loan that the Expos will repay over a given period. . . ."

Montreal mayor Jean Doré was then consulted. He also wanted to keep the Expos in Montreal, and his enthusiasm was even greater than Bourassa's. Beyond economic considerations, he saw the Expos as a prestigious asset for the city. But Doré also thought Montrealers would never accept direct government assistance unless it were limited and temporary. At any rate, Major League Baseball would never allow a city to become co-owner of a team. For that reason, our group was required to issue special type "B" shares, nonparticipating and nonvoting, especially for the City of Montreal.

The city would boast of special status among the investors and would be first in line to recoup its investment before any other partner could sell its shares and leave the consortium. But Montreal's participation wasn't to be permanent. As the general partner, I committed to finding buyers for these shares. I found only one, Paul Roberge of Boutiques San Francisco, who reduced the city's share by $2 million.

Mayor Doré then contacted Mario Bertrand, Premier Bourassa's chief of staff, to let him know the city was going ahead and would publicly announce its intention to invest in the Expos. "Will you do the same?" Doré asked.

"Yes," Bertrand immediately answered.

The Quebec government and the City of Montreal therefore agreed to commit $18 million and $15 million, respectively, to the purchase of the Expos. For me, it was a critical first step, one Ménard and I had successfully completed.

Now it was the private sector's turn. There was no way we'd borrow the necessary funds from banking institutions. I wanted the owners to participate through the injection of debt-free capital, so as not to mortgage the franchise's future. This capital would be invested by the partners themselves within the framework of a limited partnership. With the exception of the SDI, which would supply a loan, each associate—including the City of Montreal—would receive an ownership share in the Expos proportionate to its financial participation.

Jerry Reinsdorf and his committee approved this first-step agreement.

The selling price had yet to be determined. After first establishing it at $85 million, Vineberg and Rabinovitch, Bronfman's advisors, revised their evaluation upward. Expansion had been talked about for some time, and Wayne Huizenga of Florida, among others, hoped to get a ball club. No doubt Bronfman, who was already being approached, could have gotten that asking price from the Americans. And much more. An offer of $150 million was even submitted to the Expos' owner. Given the situation, Vineberg and Rabinovitch fixed the selling price for the team at $100 million.

After deducting the debt accumulated over the years ($44 million), Bronfman would yield an annual return of about seven percent on his initial $10 million investment. Not much, but he hadn't become involved in baseball solely for financial reasons. This figure nevertheless allowed him to get back his initial outlay, settle the debt, and yield a modest return.

In February 1990, during training camp in West Palm Beach, Bronfman officially announced his club was for sale. From that moment on, he slowly but surely withdrew from the management of the ball club. He'd always given me plenty of room to manoeuvre; this time, though, he pulled away completely. It was the same story at the Major League Baseball level. Bronfman stopped attending the owners meetings. I took over.

The mandate of the Ownership Committee is to protect the interests of all Major League Baseball owners. By vetting each transaction, it aims to ensure no new owner comes along to tarnish or compromise the reputation (financial or otherwise) of the two leagues. It also wants to ensure any new owner will fit in with Major League Baseball's management philosophy and maintain harmonious relations with the other owners.

As I have mentioned, even if the owners weren't directly affected by the sale of the Expos, they were hardly indifferent to it. Quite the opposite. At the end of the day, they were the ones who had to either approve or reject the deal.

The presence of the team's president in the group of owners reassured them. It was proof the transaction would be concluded smoothly. I chaired several committees; they knew me well. In their eyes, even if the club wasn't yet officially sold, I'd already succeeded Bronfman. From then on, I'd run the ball club.

After several months of hard work, Ménard, his team, and I had all the elements in hand to convince the private sector to get involved in the purchase of the Expos. The participation of both the Quebec government and the City of Montreal had been confirmed, and Major League Baseball had approved Burns Fry's confidential information memorandum.

I was confident. The acquisition of the Expos was good business. The cost of obtaining a baseball franchise had risen rapidly over the previous few years as a result of increased demand from prospective American buyers, multimillionaires who considered the acquisition of a professional sports team to be a sound investment. I was convinced the increase in the cost of a franchise wasn't about to stop, especially in the prevailing context of league expansion.

Compared with the resources of these multimillionaires, no Quebec company could measure up. But, as it happened, Bronfman didn't want to sell the Expos to Americans. Once again it was a sentimental decision, one that cost him several million dollars.

Obviously, baseball's situation in Montreal was hardly as bright as it was in American cities. But I was optimistic. I was certain Montrealers would reconnect with their team sooner or later. The Expos were an excellent organization, the envy of other teams in Major League Baseball. There was no doubt the quality of the organization would soon help to convince fans to come and cheer on their team. Even if, in the worst-case scenario, fans continued to steer clear, new buyers would have no trouble reselling the franchise to American interests for an amount much higher than the original cost of acquisition. The purchase of the Expos was therefore a no-risk investment that would interest several Quebec companies.

I was so convinced it was good business I didn't hesitate to invest everything I had. I also wanted to reassure potential investors. If I myself believed in it (enough to risk everything), I could better convince the others of the seriousness of the enterprise.

I had a considerable income as president of the Expos, but it wasn't enough to join the ranks of the private investors. So I turned to Bronfman and made a proposal. He'd keep the sales commission he'd promised me ($500,000) and, in return, lend me $1 million, interest free, for five years. And another $1 million— this time with interest—also for five years. With $2 million in my pocket, I could get on board.

The risk was great, especially because I had to put up my home as collateral for the loan from Bronfman. Several of my friends advised me not to get involved. "You'll lose your shirt," they told me. But I was confident. I was convinced my investment would be profitable. Not only mine but also those of all the investors who'd join the consortium. The bill was high. For about five years, I paid $8,000 to $9,000 a month in interest. I took a very big risk.

We required a minimum investment of $5 million from each private sector investor, an amount that seemed realistic to both Expos' management and the Burns Fry team. Jacques Ménard, Jean Lajoie, and I got to work and contacted dozens of private firms. Among them was Power Corporation, which had refused

Bronfman's initial offer but might accept becoming part of a group of shareholders. And there were many others: Bombardier, Desjardins, Unimédia, Provigo, les Pharmacies Jean Coutu, les Rotisseries St-Hubert, Vidéotron, Imperial Tobacco, les Fromageries Saputo. . . . All the major companies in Quebec and several in Ontario were approached.

The answer was the same every time. "No, thank you."

The excuses varied from one firm to the other. Power Corporation's Paul Desmarais admitted he knew nothing about baseball and "preferred hockey anyway." Jacques Francoeur of Unimédia said he was too old to embark on such an adventure. "If only I were 10 years younger," he told the media. Bertin Nadeau, president of Unigesco and Provigo, wanted to "let others have the opportunity." Jean Coutu, for his part, found the purchase price too high. Québécor's Pierre Péladeau judged that, with $4 million a year in profits, the company wasn't profitable enough. Even Raymond Malenfant, then an extremely wealthy hotelier, declined the offer. He said "no Quebecer had the financial wherewithal to buy the Expos, except Charles Bronfman."

I was surprised. Apparently, what seemed obvious to me wasn't nearly as obvious to others. In hindsight, though, I could understand the initial reaction from the private sector. Since the beginning, the Expos had belonged to one man. No one knew the business very well—not to mention the game of baseball itself. As well, from a public relations point of view, the team was poorly perceived. There wasn't the familiarity—in the good sense of the word—between the Expos and Quebecers (which included the directors of these large companies) that existed between the Montreal Canadiens, for example, and Quebecers.

Not that this prevented baseball from being very popular in Montreal at that time. The Expos played twice as many games as the Canadiens did, and at each game there were as many people as at a hockey game—sometimes more. At the end of the year, twice as many people had attended an Expos game compared to a Canadiens game.

Another element might have explained the negative response from potential investors: visibility. Bronfman was fond of saying that, when Seagrams acquired Tropicana Juices or Martell cognacs for several billion dollars, he received brief mentions in the business sections of newspapers. But when the Expos traded Tim Raines, the impact was major—and sometimes very negative.

Most businesspeople prefer to run their companies far from the bright lights. By getting involved in the Expos, they'd be exposed to publicity that wasn't always the right kind. If the club wins, so much the better. But when it loses, the name of the company is associated with the poor performance of the team. Molson would feel that impact once the Canadiens stopped being perennial champions.

To a certain extent, I understood the business community's reticence. But what I deplored was that their comments found their way into the media. It was as though each company felt the need to justify its refusal. The discretion required in this type of deal was difficult to maintain. The representatives of these companies didn't hesitate to vilify the project at every turn. Such vilification, obviously, complicated our efforts.

For the journalists, there was no doubt that the future of the Expos was in jeopardy and that the team's moving was a possible, if not a probable, solution. Nothing there, either, to inspire the confidence of potential investors.

And, if that weren't enough, along came Hugh Hallward, one of the members of the Expos' Board of Directors and a minority owner of the team with Bronfman. Hallward confided to reporters he'd recommended to his friends not to get involved. His argument? In 1990, the Canadian dollar was overevaluated. It was expected to drop to 80¢ U.S. in short order. How would the Expos manage to pay the salaries of the players?

Hallward's statements were stunning. A fervent Expos fan, Bronfman's partner since the beginning, Hallward also appeared to be tired of the whole thing. He was ready to move on, which may have explained his defeatism. All the more because he also said that, if he were 20 years old, he probably wouldn't have reacted the same way.

His comments infuriated me, even if he was right about the Canadian dollar—which dropped not to 80¢ U.S. but to . . . 63¢. But it's not good for business to have a seller who recommends to potential buyers not to buy.

Attacked from all quarters, the consortium project was struggling. While Ménard, his team, and I continued our efforts, the ball club tried hard to keep the commitments it had already acquired: the City of Montreal and the Quebec government. We reassured them by telling them that companies were interested. We also tried to stall Bronfman.

At the end of July 1990, six months after the announcement of the intention to sell, not a single private investor had come forward in a serious way. Bronfman hoped the team would stay in Quebec, but there were limits to his patience. To get things moving, and to help us as well, he publicly established a deadline: September 1.

I turned to Labatt Breweries, which had always supported the Expos. I proposed the company immediately renew its sponsorship, to the tune of $35 million over five years. Labatt agreed, and we quickly convened reporters to announce the news.

Same scenario with Petro-Canada. Three days after Labatt's decision, Petro-Canada signed a $16 million deal for the next four years.

Little by little, the winds shifted. The business world became aware the Expos had a future. There already were guaranteed revenues. Perhaps the business wasn't so bad after all.

Montreal was talking about it. Among boards of directors, in management committee meetings, even on the golf courses—everywhere businesspeople got together—the Expos were discussed. Not as a potentially profitable investment but as a necessity for the growth of Montreal. We have to help the Expos; the team has to stay here. . . .

Reassured by the financial commitments from Labatt and Petro-Canada, which wanted to make concrete gestures toward the city, companies that had been approached began to review their positions.

Canadian Pacific's Bill Stinson, a good friend of mine, called me and said, "Claude, if Bell gets on board, I will too." So Ménard set up a meeting with Bell's Raymond Cyr. It wasn't the first time we'd approached Cyr. We practically had to get down on our knees each time, but Cyr always hesitated. On this day, no begging was necessary; he'd made his decision. Cigar in his mouth, an amused look on his face, he joked, "Listen. I'm prepared to make a *donation*. Five million. But on one condition: that you never bother me about it again! Understood? *Never*." Everyone burst out laughing.

The decisions by these two investors warmed up other companies to the idea. Desjardins manifested its interest, as did the Fédération des travailleurs du Québec (FTQ)'s Solidarity Fund. Bombardier as well, but with one major condition: that the government not be part of the consortium. It was an unacceptable caveat given the commitments of Robert Bourassa and Jean Doré, but Ménard and I nevertheless accepted the letter of intent from Laurent Beaudoin. André Bérard agreed to commit Banque Nationale, on the condition the shareholders' group not be a limited partnership. Another unacceptable stipulation, but we didn't refuse the participation of this new partner, telling ourselves he might soften his position when the group was complete.

The commitments from Bombardier and Banque Nationale, added to those of Bell, Desjardins, and Canadian Pacific, showed the project was moving in the right direction. Soon other companies appeared: Avie Bennett of McClelland & Stewart was ready to supply between $2.5 million and $5 million; Provigo and Télémédia agreed to invest $5 million each. Including my share ($2 million) and the Burns Fry sales commission Ménard wanted to invest in the purchase ($1 million), our group found itself with between $45.5 and $48 million in commitments.

Other companies and individuals were also approached and could eventually invest: Alcan, CN, Conrad Black, Gaz Métropolitain, Maxwell Communications, Domtar, the Loeb family of

Ottawa. And perhaps even Petro-Canada, which had just signed a new sponsorship agreement with us. In all, $35–$40 million from potential investors who were studying the proposal.

During the next few months, companies travelled from one list to the other, from those "confirmed" to those "undecided." We made up those lists to convince ourselves we were further along than we really were. We showed them to potential investors, we told them that this company had said yes, that another one was very interested, and so on.

The deadline set by Bronfman had long passed, but the Expos' owner remained patient. At any rate, everything bode well despite the song and dance we were getting from some of the companies.

Coca-Cola Canada wanted to invest, but final approval wasn't granted at the head office in Atlanta. No matter. The company still wanted to commit. It signed an exclusive sponsorship contract for $5 million. An enormous sum compared with what Coca-Cola normally would have paid. Less than a million, in my estimation.

Ménard and I worked flat out. We made progress slowly, painfully. Coca-Cola's decision rallied the investors even more; the list of "confirmed" lengthened little by little. But nothing was assured.

That's when Claude Blanchet of the Solidarity Fund and Guy Langlois of Provigo came into the picture.

CHAPTER 3

Ten Dollars, "Just in Case You Need It . . ."

Claude Blanchet and Guy Langlois were formidable deal makers.

The Solidarity Fund typically buys businesses and invests in the share capital of a wide variety of companies, and Blanchet and his team were masters in the art of the deal. It was the same for Langlois at Provigo, a major Quebec supermarket chain.

These seasoned negotiators were under the impression the current negotiating team, Jacques Ménard and I, didn't have enough of an iron grip to bring the operation to a successful conclusion. According to them, I was poorly positioned to negotiate the best deal because I was both a buyer and a seller. And, once again according to them, Ménard had but one objective: to finalize the sale as quickly as possible and get his hands on his commission.

Blanchet and Langlois decided to take matters in their own hands, despite our opposition. Without our knowledge, they met privately with the heads of companies that did business with the Expos. For example, they began negotiating with the Olympic Installations Board to reduce the Expos' operating costs, generate new revenues, and extract more generous participation from the provincial government.

OIB president Pierre Bibeau was the consortium's best ally with Premier Robert Bourassa. Attempting to reduce or even eliminate the rent paid to the OIB didn't seem, to him, to be the right approach. The government was pushing the board to increase its revenues. And here we were, once again trying to squeeze the board with our demands after the last rent reduction had already chilled the relationship between the two parties. I'd gone over the head of Bibeau's predecessor and directly to the premier's office to settle all that; I'd negotiated the Expos' new lease agreement with the premier's chief of staff, Mario Bertrand. It had taken two years for the OIB to forgive me for that one. The OIB absolutely had to come out a winner in the new agreement, but Blanchet and Langlois were making things difficult.

I wasn't too hard on the two men. I understood their impatience and their eagerness to get the best possible deal—not only for themselves but also for the other members of the group, which included Ménard and me. But it was annoying and rather tiresome to watch them go at it.

Soon the search for partners hit a wall.

We couldn't have met their demands in any case, but a progress report presented by Burns Fry revealed that Banque Nationale and Bombardier had decided to pull out of the consortium. The Loeb family of Ottawa had also decided to withdraw. Maxwell Communications too.

The loss of these investors was like a bucket of cold water being poured on us, and it required the rest of the group to reevaluate the action plan. The situation wasn't moving forward; what could we do to get it back on track?

I telephoned Charles Bronfman. "It's not working," I said. "We'll have to look elsewhere."

"An American?" he asked.

"One who wouldn't be the major shareholder, of course, but who might be able to make up the difference for the Canadian investors."

"Even if he were the majority owner, it wouldn't be a problem. As long as he commits to keeping the club in Montreal. Do you have anyone in mind?" Bronfman asked.

"Maybe. Martin Stone. The owner of the Phoenix Firebirds, a triple-A team. He called me; he is interested . . . ," I said.

Not only was Stone a baseball fan, but he also owned a huge ranch near Lake Placid, less than two hours from Montreal in up-state New York.

In October 1990, this gentleman farmer arrived in Montreal to meet with me. Stone seemed to be prepared to invest several million dollars, which would have allowed the group to complete the transaction. His presence had another advantage. In contrast to my Canadian partners, Stone knew the baseball business. I felt a little less alone with him on board.

One thing was certain. The arrival of this American millionaire reassured some of the other buyers in the consortium, who finally foresaw a solution to their problems. Avie Bennett of McClelland & Stewart, on the other hand, wasn't very enthusiastic. He wanted the consortium to be completely Canadian.

For several weeks, through numerous meetings, discussions with Stone continued to determine the size of his investment and the role he'd play in the team's management. He made it clear that, if he supplied the largest amount of capital, he intended to control the ball club.

One day Langlois was at the board in the conference room, marker in hand, making a list of the confirmed amounts. He turned toward Stone. "How about you, Martin? How much are you ready to invest?" he asked.

Stone had never mentioned a specific amount, but we were under the impression he'd be ready to go up to $20 million.

"So, Martin. How much?" Langlois insisted.

"One million in cash. . . ."

Dead silence. We all looked at each other confusedly. One measly little million! We were way off.

"But I'll throw in the value of my Firebirds," Stone added once he saw the looks on the faces of his future partners.

Maximum $6 or $7 million. And most of it wasn't cash. In any case, it was too little to take control of the team.

We dismissed Stone and went looking for another backer. One wasted no time in coming forward. In a few years, he'd become familiar to every baseball fan in Montreal. His name was Jeffrey Loria.

A fabulously wealthy art dealer from New York, Loria was already the owner—as Stone was—of a triple-A team, this one in Oklahoma City. And, like Stone, he'd always dreamed of owning a major-league baseball team.

Ménard, his financial advisor Joel Mael, the others, and I met with Loria on several occasions. But the discussions led nowhere. Loria wanted complete control of the team, something the partners—and especially I—wouldn't grant him.

During the course of this hunt for investors, it had always been understood I'd remain president of the team. Loria was ready to keep me on board, but he'd have moved me to a position without any real authority—a position that, in any case, would have been only temporary.

I quickly understood this man negotiated only one way: his way. He was both a hardnosed and an affable man, convinced of one thing only: that he was always right. An iron fist in a velvet glove.

Loria's financial proposal was rejected. Maybe next time. The American multimillionaire kept the Expos' phone number in his Rolodex.

Throughout the 1990s, I tried to put a group together to buy back the City of Montreal's share of the Expos, evaluated at $13 million. It was in this context that I once again got in touch with Loria. But the buyback plan was abandoned. We wouldn't hear of Loria—and his iron fist—again until 1998.

Ménard and I put the Americans aside and once again began approaching Quebec companies. It was complicated, discouraging at times, especially since Bronfman wasn't making our lives any easier.

Two of the buyers annoyed Bronfman to no end. The first was Claude Blanchet of the Solidarity Fund. As it was, Bronfman wasn't happy to see a financial organization tied to a labour union become part of the consortium. Neither, for that matter, was Major League Baseball. It was prepared to tolerate the Québécois "difference," but the fact that a team might be purchased by both a municipality and a union made its executives extremely uneasy. Such a situation would be unacceptable in the United States.

Mostly, it was Blanchet's personality that upset Bronfman. Composed, thoughtful, endeavouring to carry on his business with the greatest discretion, Bronfman was irritated by the rash declarations from Blanchet, who never hesitated to use the media to criticize Bronfman's intransigence about the selling price. Bronfman knew he could let the club go to the United States for far more money. By selling it for $100 million, he was giving the Canadian partners a good deal. There was no question of his giving in on that point and even less reason to criticize him for it.

The situation gradually simmered down. Thankfully so, because we needed the Solidarity Fund.

The second investor rejected by Bronfman was Pierre Péladeau. Raymond Lemay, one of Péladeau's closest advisors, had contacted me to evaluate the potential participation in the partnership of Péladeau's company, Québécor. But Péladeau had found himself in hot water after making statements judged to be anti-Semitic. Bronfman told me, clearly and simply, not to include Québécor in the group of buyers. The message was relayed to Lemay; nothing more was said.

In spite of Bronfman's dislike of Blanchet and Péladeau, and in spite of our refusal to associate ourselves with Americans and risk losing control of the team, Ménard and I managed—with great difficulty—to get firm commitments of about $85 million, an amount that included the participation of the Quebec government and the City of Montreal.

We weren't there yet, but Bronfman and I judged the time had come to submit the sales proposal to Major League Baseball to garner its support.

On November 3, 1990, Bronfman, Ménard, and I flew to Dallas, where baseball's Ownership Committee was convening. Our work was well received by committee members as well as National League president Bill White and Major League Baseball commissioner Fay Vincent, Bud Selig's predecessor.

Among those present, the owner of the Texas Rangers wondered about the Expos' precarious financial situation. His name? George W. Bush, the future president of the United States. I knew him well. We had one major thing in common: he, too, had invested everything he had in his team. And he'd been a member of the owners "club" for just over two years. As rookies amid veterans, we'd become good friends. It wasn't unusual to see Bush arrive at ownership meetings wearing cowboy boots, each adorned with a miniature map of Texas.

"It won't work, your deal," Bush said.

"Trust me," I replied.

"I'd like to, but see things as they are. You don't have enough money."

"We have the lowest payroll in the league."

"So what? You'll be in the red in less than two years. . . ."

I disagreed. I had specific ideas on how to manage the club. I was sure the Expos could become a formidable team, even with limited financial resources.

Bush's doubts were shared by the other members of the committee, who found the consortium lacked money. The buyers had no manoeuvring room to ensure the viability of the club. They therefore asked Ménard and I to find $10 million more.

I was disappointed by their response. But at least the proposed structure had been accepted. The Americans had a hard time accepting the participation of the City of Montreal—even less that of the Solidarity Fund—but I told them once again that there was no alternative in the Quebec context.

Over the next few weeks, I tried to convince the owners to approve my buyout project. I worked on putting the finishing touches on the deal and—most of all—on increasing the financial participation of each of the investors and finding new ones.

The negotiations with Bronfman and his sales team were far from complete. At the end of November, Bronfman, Vineberg, and Rabinovitch met with Ménard, Blanchet, Langlois, the others, and me. There'd been new capital contributions but also the withdrawal of some partners; the result was that there remained a $10 million gap between seller and buyers.

That was when Blanchet proposed to make up the $10 million in the form of game tickets. Each year for 10 years, 200,000 tickets worth five dollars each would be given to charity in Bronfman's name so underprivileged youngsters could attend Expos games.

The negotiations continued over several days. Finally, an agreement in principle was reached. On November 29, 1990, after a long and arduous night of negotiating, the telephone rang in my office. It was 10:30 a.m.

"Claude, it's the former Expos' owner talking to you. . . ."

I couldn't even answer, so shaken was I by the news. This was it. After months of relentless work, after narrowly averting failure on several occasions, I'd met the challenge of keeping the team in Montreal.

It was a very emotional moment. As a former military man, I'm not inclined to let my feelings show. But that day, in my office, I sat still for a long time, shaken by the news, trying to put my thoughts—and my emotions—into some kind of order.

That very morning I'd received a letter that had moved me to tears. A young fan, eight-year-old Jerome Miller, had written to me to offer his support, saying we *had* to save the Expos. Slipped into the envelope was a $10 bill and a note: "Just in case you need it. . . ." I was already imagining Jerome's joy, the joy of all the team's fans. The Expos had been saved.

CHAPTER 4

"Are You Comfortable with This?"

The following afternoon, I called a press conference at Olympic Stadium.

In a choked voice, with Jacques Ménard and me at his sides, Charles Bronfman confirmed the sale of the Expos to the new consortium.

To the media and the public, Ménard and I were the heroes of the day. Several journalists who'd never believed the team would survive had to face the facts. A new era was dawning for the Expos because of our efforts and the financial participation of Quebec companies and the various levels of government.

Over the course of that winter, while Major League Baseball evaluated the transaction, I worked on meeting the requirements of several partners, Télémédia among them. The media company had agreed to get involved on the condition the amount raised from other partners add up to at least $55 million, which wasn't yet the case. To get Télémédia on board, Jocelyn Proteau of Caisses Populaires Desjardins and Claude Blanchet of the Solidarity Fund agreed to increase their investments from $5 million to $7 million apiece.

Another partner joined them. I originally met Mark Routtenberg, who'd made his money in plumbing (he'd just sold his company, Ideal Plumbing), through a fund-raising campaign he ran for Sun Youth, a local charity. During a meal together, I asked him if he were interested in becoming part of the consortium. He was. He invested $2 million in the Expos through his company, Freemark Investments. Routtenberg would later acquire Guess Jeans.

Over the years, my wife, Michelle, and I became good friends with Mark and Frema Routtenberg. But our friendship came to an abrupt end when, several years later, Routtenberg sided with the other partners in demanding my resignation.

On April 11, 1991, Raymond Crevier of the law firm of Ogilvy Renault greeted us at the Ritz-Carlton Hotel, where we handed him our cheques. The lawyer would deposit the cheques in trust, to be held until such time as Major League Baseball approved the transaction.

One by one, representatives from Desjardins and the Solidarity Fund ($7 million each), Provigo, Bell Canada, Canadian Pacific, Télémédia, McClelland & Stewart Sports, and vs Services (which each contributed $5 million to the consortium) filed past Crevier. The other partners were also present. Cascades, Freemark Investments, and I added $2 million each. Burns Fry invested $1 million, its commission on the deal.

I'd never personally made out a cheque for such a large amount. Two million dollars. I had butterflies in my stomach.

In all, $51 million, to which we added the $5 million paid by Coca-Cola for exclusivity rights. With the $33 million contributed by the City of Montreal and the Quebec government (through the sdi), the consortium had put together a total of $89 million to purchase the club.

In legal terms, we formed a limited partnership headed by one partner, called the general partner. I'd run the team in the name of all the other associates.

The deal was far from being finalized. For the next two months, three men examined every aspect of the partnership agreement in detail: Fred Kuhlmann of the St. Louis Cardinals, on behalf of the Ownership Committee; Tom Ostertag, legal counsel for the commissioner's office; and Bob Kheel of the National League's legal department. They cut the proposed deal to pieces; their job was to purge it of any undesirable elements until it conformed to the standards set out by the Ownership Committee.

It was hardly the first time Kuhlmann had examined the transfer of power from one owner to another. But the Montreal case was unique because of the presence of multiple partners and of an organization with union ties, the Solidarity Fund.

The Ownership Committee wanted to ensure the general partner truly had the authority to make decisions without having to get approval from the other partners. It was a condition essential to the ratification of the deal by Major League Baseball. As well, in all cases of ownership transfer where the buyer was a limited partnership, the Ownership Committee required that the general partner be the sole spokesperson for the team. It wanted to negotiate with a single representative—particularly in the case of a group as heterogeneous as the one attempting to buy the Expos.

In the early drafts of the contract, however, the partners proposed a level of control over the general partner Kuhlmann deemed excessive. He therefore insisted on the modification of certain clauses to afford me more protection.

Major League Baseball went even further. The commissioner had a clause added stipulating Major League Baseball must approve any change in the general partner. The other members of the consortium therefore couldn't replace me without the endorsement of the commissioner. When all was said and done, I could be fired only for fraud or financial mismanagement.

It was an important clause that would have major repercussions a few years later. But back in 1991, all the partners accepted the terms of the contract, even though they obviously would have preferred to be able to exert more control over the organization.

During the negotiations, the relationship between Major League Baseball and the consortium was excellent. Kuhlmann and his team took great care to make the partners understand the reasons behind the inclusion of those clauses in the agreement. Everyone understood the transaction would not be ratified unless the Ownership Committee was satisfied and had confidence in the buyers.

At any rate, the requirements of Major League Baseball weren't delivered all at once. Little by little, as we went along, on one side as much as on the other, we arrived at these proposals. Kuhlmann would often turn to me. "Are you comfortable with this?" he would ask.

If I said no, he reworked the clause to ensure that, as the control partner, the man whom he would be dealing with, I had the necessary authority to run the club.

On several occasions, Kuhlmann reassured me. "Don't worry, Claude. We'll take care of you," he said.

I was one of them, obviously; they knew me well. There was no question of leaving me in Montreal without protection or in a position of weakness vis-à-vis my partners.

It was a stressful period. I was concerned a company or individual would balk at Major League Baseball's requirements and pull out of the consortium. That would have been a disaster. Fortunately, everyone remained on board.

At that point, the various partners' marketing departments took over. They wanted to derive maximum benefit for their companies on the marketing end. Desjardins asked for exclusivity on financial services. Bell asked for the same in telecommunications. Télémédia wanted the French-language radio broadcast rights. Versa Foods wanted the concessions. And so on. Not to mention the complimentary tickets some of the partners were asking for.

Finally, on June 12, 1991, in Santa Monica, California, the owners of the National and American Leagues approved the transaction.

In my opinion, there were several reasons for the success of the operation. The commitment of the investors and the unwavering support of the provincial government and the municipal administration certainly played a role. The federal government also contributed by giving tax breaks to the investors. As well, Bronfman and his associates were prepared to reduce the selling price to keep the Expos in Montreal. And Major League Baseball supported the efforts of the local investors, who could take advantage of the expertise and competence of the Expos' management team.

When new investors bought out the team in 1999, those winning conditions no longer existed. With the results we are all aware of. . . .

Some of my partners didn't understand what a limited partnership really meant—particularly where the role of the general partner was concerned. They had signed the partnership agreement without truly grasping its significance. They tended to establish a parallel with what had happened with the Quebec Nordiques. A few years before, well-known lawyer Marcel Aubut headed up a group of investors vying to buy the hockey club from its former owner, O'Keefe Breweries. In his agreement with his partners, Aubut made sure he'd run the club as he saw fit; he answered to no one. The buyers of the Expos didn't want to repeat this mistake. They were concerned I would become another Aubut, ignoring them and doing as I pleased. They asked for the right to closely scrutinize their investment in the club.

An executive committee was formed, as provided for in the partnership agreement. The investors voted in Jacques Ménard, Jocelyn Proteau of Desjardins, Claude Blanchet of the Solidarity Fund, and Jacques Bérubé of Bell. It was, of course, a committee without any decision-making power, and it wouldn't last very long. Proteau and Blanchet didn't want to limit themselves to a purely advisory role. I prepared myself for some stormy times at the helm of the good ship Expos.

But for the moment, at least, the relationship between my partners and me was still full of promise. Major League Baseball had approved our initiative. And I could now go back to what I loved doing most: running a baseball team and leading it to the top.

CHAPTER 5

A Top-Rank Team

Columnist Michael Farber of the Montreal *Gazette* considered the purchase of the Expos by a primarily francophone group of Quebecers as yet more evidence of the anglophone community's diminishing importance in Montreal. "English Montreal gently gives way to French Montreal, again," he wrote. "And the thrills and disappointments will belong to others."

Anglophone attendance at Expos games had dropped slowly but progressively over the years. During a meeting with two of the *Gazette*'s top editors, Joan Fraser and David Alnutt, Vice President of Marketing and Communications Richard Morency and I tried to gain some understanding of the anglophones' negative reaction toward the "new" Expos. We considered several reasons, but it appeared anglophone fans might have been reacting to the Expos in the same way they reacted to Steinberg when that company was sold to francophone Michel Gaucher. They stopped shopping at Steinberg because, in their minds, the supermarket chain no longer "belonged" to them.

Yet even francophones were no longer cheering for their team as much as they had, and this drop in attendance created a major financial headache for the team's executives. To get through this difficult period, I needed either to find fresh sources of financing or to draw on the team's reserves. But even the latter wasn't a solution; we had no reserves.

In previous years, Charles Bronfman had never hesitated to

either absorb the club's debts or ensure bridge financing in a timely manner. But the situation had changed with the arrival of the new owners. Those who'd just invested their millions weren't about to inject additional funds—especially given their commitment wasn't a business decision as much as it was a willingness to help Montreal.

I couldn't discuss our tight financial situation with anyone. It was especially important the media not get wind the club was in trouble.

Basically, we had no way of dealing with a drop in revenue. We sometimes had to delay issuing cheques to some of our creditors because the bank accounts were, to put it bluntly, as dry as a bone. This situation persisted for several years.

How do you run a professional baseball team that way? And how do you make it the winning team called for by the media and fans? There was only one solution: to live within our means, even if doing so was sometimes frustrating for the fans. I informed the investors of my management philosophy from the beginning. I considered myself the guarantor of their commitment, and I didn't want to ruin them—or myself.

It was therefore critical to put a premium on player development. To acquire Mark Langston in 1989, we had to give up very good players who would have helped the team down the line. At this point, we no longer had those players, and Langston was long gone.

No, the only way to get out of it was to call on players developed by the organization, players from affiliated minor-league clubs scattered all over North America. At the time, they included Indianapolis, Harrisburg, West Palm Beach, Rockford, Sumter, and Jamestown. We would look to South America, to Venezuela. We also had baseball academies, notably in the Dominican Republic, whose objective was to find and develop new players.

The cycle was always the same. After his selection in the amateur draft, a young player was developed for several years in our farm system. When the coaching staff judged him ready to join the "big club," we brought him to Montreal. The player would stay with the big-league club for five or six years on average, rarely more. We had no choice. As soon as a player has spent six years in the major leagues, he can become a free agent, which allows him to shop his services to any team in either league.

In the case of our best players, we didn't have the means to match an offer from a U.S.-based team. As a result, those players would leave the organization. We received young players in the draft as compensation, and the cycle would begin anew. For four or five years, the new team would improve little by little as the young players gained experience. And at the end of that period, we once again had a team capable of competing for top spot with the other teams in the National League.

With the exception of the trade that brought Langston to Montreal, we had generally operated this way—not by choice but out of financial necessity. And in the future, given our precarious situation, the lack of financing, and the decline in value of the Canadian dollar versus its U.S. counterpart, we would be constrained to follow the same development model.

All of which didn't mean the team was of lesser value. Quite the opposite. Many squads had to deal with blasé, lavishly paid players; we could count on talented, enthusiastic, young athletes who had everything to prove.

My other decision was to sign only short-term contracts with the players; long-term deals were to be reserved for exceptional cases. As much as possible, we limited ourselves to renewable one-year deals, especially during the player's arbitration-eligible period. We couldn't afford to find ourselves backed into a corner by a player whose salary would increase at a much faster rate than our ability to pay it.

Following the same logic, we tried to quickly trade away players whose performance was disappointing. Once again the idea was to acquire young players who would undergo rigorous development over the next few years with one of our farm clubs.

Because of this difficult financial context, one that deprived us of big names and rendered us unable to compete with other teams on the free-agent market, we had to pay far more attention to our farm system than did the wealthier teams to theirs. For most of those teams, player development is just one element among many, since they have the means to take advantage of the free-agent market. We didn't have that luxury. We therefore put all of our energies and all of our resources into establishing strong, well-structured, minor-league organizations that boasted the best coaches in baseball. The staff we hired was the envy of the other major-league clubs.

What our organization put into practice was the good, old-fashioned method of managing a baseball club, one that had been the norm before the advent of free agency. We had little money, but we spent more on development than the average organization. The results were stunning. Often our organization was voted the best in baseball.

With Dave Dombrowski as general manager, Bill Stoneman as vice president of baseball operations, and Eddie Haas as executive advisor, the Expos were every bit as good as any other team. Same thing in terms of player development. Farm Director Kevin Kennedy, Director of Scouting Kevin Malone, Director of Latin American and International Scouting Fred Ferreira, and their many lieutenants, including David Littlefield and Ed Creech, made up one of the most competent and experienced groups in the game.

Unfortunately, they never received the recognition they deserved from either the Montreal media or the public. Even as all of Major League Baseball regularly congratulated us on our organization, the envy of many other cities on the circuit, it was judged inadequate and unsuccessful in our own backyard.

In 1991, in an article entitled "Organizations of First Rank," *The Sporting News* deemed our farm system the best in professional baseball, far outranking those of the Los Angeles Dodgers and the New York Yankees. "The Montreal Expos, reaping the benefits from several years of heavy drafting, rank No. 1," the article stated. "They are several notches ahead of the second-ranked Dodgers and the third-ranked Yankees, two longtime rich organizations that had fallen on lean times in the 1980s." The magazine also placed six of our prospects among the 75 most promising minor-league players in the game. We were second in that category behind the San Francisco Giants, who boasted seven.

What's more, three of the club's farm teams won championships in their respective leagues: West Palm Beach (Florida State League), Jamestown (New York-Penn League), and Bradenton (Gulf Coast League). Another team, the Harrisburg Senators, reached the Eastern League championship final.

So it was hardly surprising the team's on-field performance was remarkable. Only twice since 1979 (in 1984 and 1986) had we failed to end the season with a record above .500. In addition, the ball club won its division during the strike-shortened season of 1981.

But we couldn't expect to win regularly and repeatedly, because our success depended on the young players' development cycle. I explained this management philosophy, which sometimes could be frustrating for the fans, in painstaking detail to the other members of the limited partnership.

During a meeting on December 16, 1991, for example, I outlined the team's situation in terms of finances, player contracts, and radio and television broadcast rights in the United States. I also tackled other areas, such as the relationship between the Expos and the Olympic Installations Board, the concessions, ticket sales, security, and so on. I also tried to help the other partners understand the reasons for our success, notably the player scouting and development systems. I tried to convey to them my pride in this system.

Unfortunately, most of the members of the consortium didn't give a damn about the details, despite their substantial investments in the team. Other than Mark Routtenberg, a true Expos fan, the representatives of the corporate partners had little interest in baseball. No one seemed to care about the context in which I operated. The partners seemed to think it was easy—and completely normal— to have a winning major-league team and one of the best scouting and player development departments in the game.

At the end of the 1992 training camp, the Solidarity Fund's Claude Blanchet approached me and said, "What do you mean, a two-year contract for Tim Wallach? You're not even following your own philosophy."

"Quite the opposite," I replied, explaining to Blanchet the salary paid to Wallach was high but still reasonable given the organization's resources. Besides, Wallach could still bring a lot to the team.

Despite their lack of interest in the game, the partners backed my approach. The minutes of a meeting held on September 14, 1993, confirmed the shareholders' support for the team's general philosophy.

In running the club, I tried hard to give my staff all the latitude they needed. Had I interfered with the general manager's job, for example, I would have become an integral part of any problem and would have lost objectivity in the face of any conflicts or failures that might have resulted. Knowing they had management's support, the young general managers could acquire experience within the operating framework I had established. That is not to say, however, I was indifferent to suggestions from people who worked with me.

And sometimes I would get involved. For example, at the 1991 training camp, I asked Dombrowski to trade Otis Nixon. It wasn't that I didn't like Nixon—quite the contrary. But I believed that, by platooning him in centre field with Marquis Grissom, Manager Buck Rodgers was inhibiting Grissom's development. As a general rule, though, I preferred to stay far away from those kinds of decisions.

By June 1991, Dombrowski was convinced the Expos couldn't be successful under Rodgers, who'd managed the ball club since 1985. Dombrowski was responsible for all of the team's baseball-related activities, including trades, but Rodgers managed the Expos on the field. He'd posted more wins (520) than any manager in Expos history. As well, he was very popular with the media and the fans.

But Dombrowski couldn't forget the disastrous end to the 1989 season, when Buck was unable to motivate his troops after the all-star break. Dombrowski wanted to win, and he was certain we couldn't win with Rodgers at the helm.

As well, their personalities were incompatible. Dombrowski was rigid, meticulous, organized, and straight as an arrow; Rodgers was a *bon vivant*, a lover of fine dining. Dombrowski was young and in the first stages of a promising career. Rodgers was nearing the end of the line. Everything separated them. And in professional baseball, general managers like to surround themselves with their own people. Rodgers would never be Dombrowski's man.

Barely established in my new dual role of co-owner and general partner, I knew firing Rodgers would have major repercussions on the future of the club. Still, I approved my general manager's decision. I believed, as Dombrowski did, Buck's time had passed. But I also knew his departure would create a major storm in the media.

It was more like a tornado. As soon as the news was announced, we took a major hit from the sportswriters, who accused us of getting rid of a pillar of the team—a monument, basically. Seemingly forgotten was that Rodgers, despite his popularity and baseball knowledge, hadn't been able to bring the team to the heights everyone expected.

At the next meeting of the consortium, Avie Bennett of McClelland & Stewart stood up and said, "Claude, as the co-owners, you should have consulted us."

I was about to answer him, but Ted Graham of Versa Foods beat me to it. "In a limited partnership, Avie, you have to let the general partner do his job. You can't tie his hands. Stay out of his way."

I explained that trades, releases, all those matters were very delicate. Sometimes decisions had to be made quickly and always confidentially. All we needed was one slip of the tongue from one of the owners for there to be a leak to the media.

In the aftermath of firing Rodgers, the partners discovered their roles as investors and co-owners gave them no special access to privileged player information. The club was theirs, but they had to find out about trades through the media just like everyone else. At cocktail parties and on golf courses, they couldn't brag about knowing what was going on behind closed doors in the offices of Claude Brochu and Dave Dombrowski. Even if, officially, the relationship remained very good, I now had some very frustrated partners to deal with.

Despite this friction, and although I didn't always agree with their initiatives or stands, I treated the members of the consortium with respect and refrained from making negative public comments about them. Monique Chibok, my executive assistant, was attentive to their needs and endeavoured to fill their numerous individual requests in polite and efficient fashion. For the next eight years, my office would never waver on that front.

My position was delicate and unusual. I was the general partner, the one who headed the partnership. I was also the team's president, the one who oversaw the day-to-day activities of the club. In all of the other major-league teams run as limited partnerships, two different people filled the jobs of general partner and president.

Jacques Ménard's role was completely different. One of the first architects of the sale of the team, Ménard presided over the quarterly meetings stipulated in the partnership agreement. The other partners considered him to be the leader of the group, a role he eagerly took on. He wasted no time in appointing himself chairman of the Board of Directors even though, from a legal standpoint, that function does not exist within the framework of a limited partnership.

From the start, Ménard found himself entrusted with another responsibility: being a bridge between me and the other members of the consortium. He accompanied me to the owners meetings, even if his role was minimal. Ménard wasn't part of any Major League Baseball committee or study group since he had neither the required expertise in nor the knowledge of the issues with which Major League Baseball dealt.

Nevertheless, this function was worth an annual salary of $50,000 ($25,000 after tax), paid by the Expos. Later this amount was increased to $150,000 at the request of the partners themselves. Ménard's stipend was disbursed in the form of a leased Porsche, memberships at prestigious golf clubs, and the reimbursement of personal travel expenses. His remuneration was higher than that of the team's vice presidents, which created a certain malaise among employees subjected to a strict management policy. To try to correct this negative perception, I decided to have Ménard's salary paid by my own management company.

I had to ask my partners to stay away from the problems and controversies surrounding the baseball world. I remembered the coolness toward the Expos during the Bronfman era by the political leaders of the day. It was unthinkable to give financial aid to a team owned by a multibillionaire; at any rate, public opinion would never have allowed it. Molson dealt with the same problem with its Montreal Canadiens. Big businesses do not need any favours, people believed. Let them take the money out of their own well-oiled coffers! We were in a similar situation. A prosperous group of companies with major capital at its disposal, the consortium needed to remain discreet so as not to endanger the search for new sources of revenue.

The ball club had always negotiated issues of all kinds with the governments: tax breaks from the Ministry of Revenue, more advantageous lease arrangements with the OIB, for example. Periodically, we had to discuss issues related to immigration and health care with government authorities or practical problems such as landing rights for charter flights after the curfew imposed at Dorval Airport by the Ministry of Transport.

It was obvious, given the people who represented the Expos at these meetings were the leaders of the most prosperous and dynamic companies in Quebec, that there would be little interest in making adjustments or creating any flexibility within the existing rules. In other words, we had to continue to project the image of a team grappling with the difficulties of a small market, trying by every means possible to stay afloat. Actually, that was no image; that was the truth.

As well, for most of the members of the consortium, the Expos weren't a major concern. Jocelyn Proteau and Claude Blanchet, the representatives of Desjardins and the Solidarity Fund, understandably had more pressing issues and interests that could, at times, be at odds with those of the ball club. By flaunting themselves too openly as owners of the team, by creating the impression they controlled the club's destiny and managed it on a day-to-day basis (which wasn't the case), the partners might have placed themselves in embarrassing situations.

In 1999, René Guimond, the big boss at Télévision Quatre Saisons (TQS), was dissatisfied with the agreement proposed by Vice President of Marketing and Communications Richard Morency. He decided to approach Ménard directly to negotiate a better deal for the team's television broadcast rights. Ménard had no knowledge of this issue, knew nothing of the conditions for the renewal of television broadcast licences. Still, he committed himself to taking Guimond's request under consideration. Not surprisingly, Ménard couldn't make a deal. The result was total confusion and the absence of Expos games on TQS.

Relations with the media were equally problematic. At first, the members of the consortium agreed to address journalists via a single spokesperson, me. This agreement was soon disregarded. Sometimes, even with the best intentions, Ménard would make a statement to the press, therefore contributing to focusing attention on the consortium. It didn't really bother me because he never said anything controversial.

Mark Routtenberg of Freemark Investments also loved the cameras and microphones. I warned him on several occasions, asking him to be prudent and controlled in his statements. Each time, he promised to limit himself to official comments, but reporters had no trouble dragging confidential information out of him.

Paul Roberge of Boutiques San Francisco used his status as partner to other ends. Colourful, dynamic, overflowing with sometimes harebrained schemes to increase the Expos' popularity, Roberge knew how to get the most out of his suppliers at minimal cost, all the while ensuring the best possible visibility for his companies.

One day he suggested to me that we put up his company's advertising signs at Olympic Stadium—free of charge. "I wouldn't put them everywhere," he said, "just in the spots that haven't found a taker. If ever you sell those spaces, I'll take down my advertising. . . ."

His request seemed to be reasonable. But we had to think of the others.

"What will I tell Bell and Desjardins, who paid top dollar for similar spaces?" I asked him.

Roberge was a master in the fine art of promoting his companies and enjoying certain advantages without paying a cent. His Les Ailes de la Mode clothing-store chain never would become an Expos' corporate partner.

Despite these incidents and small hiccups along the road, the relationship between the consortium and me remained good in the first few years following acquisition of the club. The other owners gave me all the latitude I required to run the team according to the terms of the agreement approved by Major League Baseball. But, obviously, I got along better with some members than others: John Thomson and Bill Stinson of Canadian Pacific, Jim McCoubrey and Claude Beaudoin of Télémédia, Louis Tanguay of Bell, Alain Lemaire of Cascades. Ted Graham and Bob Boone of Versa Foods and Mark Routtenberg of Freemark Investments gave me unwavering support in terms of my responsibilities as president of the company.

CHAPTER 6

The Stadium Has Its Say

In early September 1991, a few months after the departure of Manager Buck Rodgers, I had to deal with another delicate situation.

One morning I received a call from Carl Barger, president of the Florida Marlins, a franchise to begin play in the National League in 1993. Barger wanted to offer our general manager, Dave Dombrowski, a job and asked me for permission to talk to him. Barger's approach was no surprise. In Major League Baseball, a team president who wants to hire away someone from an opposing club's staff must first get the green light from the president of the other team.

I could have refused Barger permission to talk to Dombrowski, and he would have had to look elsewhere. But I knew that, after spending more than three years in Montreal, Dombrowski dreamed of pursuing his career somewhere else. He would receive a much larger salary in Florida than he did in Montreal—twice as large, in fact—and would take on the challenge of building a team from scratch. On several occasions, Dombrowski had told me he was finding it more and more difficult to work within a framework of permanent budgetary restrictions.

Once he arrived in Florida, Dombrowski essentially wanted to re-create the winning team he had in Montreal. Once again Barger telephoned me. Some 15 people were eventually targeted: advisors, scouts, and even a few players.

I didn't really have a choice. Even if, technically, I could oppose the raid on my staff, I couldn't refuse my employees the opportunity to pursue their careers elsewhere under much better financial conditions. Moreover, the Marlins even offered to double some of their salaries; we didn't have the means to make counteroffers.

I wasn't discouraged by the inevitability of such a bloodletting. I knew my club and affiliates well enough to know replacements were ready, and I could let Dombrowski and the others go without weakening the team in a significant way. The gesture of the Marlins proved one thing at least: we had a remarkable organization, for which Barger was prepared to pay a premium price.

The scope of this never-before-seen initiative aroused the ire of Major League Baseball. The commissioner's office asked the Marlins to cease and desist. But the attempted raid showed the Marlins were ready to spend to ensure their club quickly became the best in the league—and they had the means to do it.

Beyond its impact on the organization, Barger's offensive was an indication the game was undergoing profound changes. The addition of new teams, the arrival of new owners even wealthier than the existing ones, and the increase in television broadcast rights in the major urban centres incited the players and their agents to demand higher salaries than ever before. It was an increase that small-revenue teams such as ours couldn't absorb. Little by little over the years, the gap had widened between the financial capabilities of teams in major centres such as the Mets, Yankees, and Dodgers and those in smaller cities such as the Pirates, Brewers, and Expos.

The situation had become untenable. In the medium term, it was a financial catastrophe. A group of owners, including me, proposed to the executives of the National League to redistribute part of the revenues of the "rich" teams, notably by increasing the compensation remitted to visiting teams, a formula already in use for many years.

When the Expos played against the New York Mets, for example, we received a small payment of 40¢ per spectator. The same thing applied when the Mets played at Olympic Stadium. This measure was a sort of contribution toward the participation of the opposing team, but it obviously favoured teams such as the Expos because we could generally expect, for example, that Shea Stadium would be more full than Olympic Stadium.

To the National League, we proposed to increase this rebate to two dollars per spectator to help the smaller-revenue teams. After much discussion, the proposal was rejected. I wasn't pleased; I thought the idea made perfect sense.

Fortunately, though, our initiative piqued the interest of other team owners. Several months later, along with the San Diego Padres, we managed to convince the Florida Marlins, Pittsburgh Pirates, and Houston Astros to band together to terminate the National League Television Agreement. This agreement, which dated back to the 1950s, authorized local teams to keep all the revenue from their radio and television broadcast rights without remitting any compensation to opposing teams. For example, each time the Expos played in New York, all the revenue from the television broadcast of the game—as long as it was on a regular network station and not on cable—went straight into the coffers of the Mets. Incredibly, because we broadcast some of our games on cable, we had to pay compensation to a team such as the Los Angeles Dodgers, which did business only with conventional broadcast networks.

The situation was unfair. On the one hand, the "rich" teams refused to allow the attendance payment to increase from 40¢ to two dollars. On the other, they kept all of their local television revenues.

Our initiative, once again, had only one goal: to increase our cash flow to be able to compete with the wealthier teams in the current context of spiralling player salaries. Everyone was shocked. No one had ever before dared to do that. The wealthier teams, as expected, reacted negatively. But the other owners and I held firm, and we decided to unilaterally withdraw from the National League Television Agreement. In practical terms, every ball club was now required to bilaterally negotiate its local television rights.

It was an impossible situation that required everyone to sit around the same table and find a solution. The absence of an agreement concerning local television affected us less than most; we earned barely $30,000 per game, while teams in major centres such as the Dodgers had revenues of up to $400,000 per game. We absolutely had to find a compromise that would satisfy everyone.

The discussions weren't easy; the Expos and our allies were treated like beggars and parasites. But the large-market teams had no choice. They had to do something, or else it would be . . . war.

After discussions extending over several months, we won our case. That led to the eventual establishment of the revenue-sharing agreement still in effect today.

Back in Montreal, the departure of Dombrowski and several other employees created a difficult situation. I wanted only one thing: to finish the season without a major problem so I could start rebuilding the team the following year.

The first season under new ownership was already a disappointment. For the first time since 1986, the team would finish the season with a sub-.500 record (.484), 29.5 games behind the leaders. A year to forget.

That was when the roof caved in—literally. On September 20, 1991, one day after hiring a new general manager (Dan Duquette), the club's vice president of operations called me in a severely agitated state. "Mr. Brochu! It's terrible," he said.

"What? What's going on?"

"A concrete beam fell off the stadium. . . ."

Olympic Stadium. The white elephant financed by Quebec taxpayers since 1976 was hardly on its first health crisis. During the season, the roof had torn. And now this girder had fallen off—fortunately without leaving any victims. Could there be any doubt the new Expos' management team was being dogged by bad luck?

And it wasn't over. André Vallerand, the minister responsible for the Olympic Installations Board, hastily declared the stadium unsafe and demanded, in the same breath, a guarantee of absolute safety before he would allow it to reopen.

The Chicago Cubs were already in town. We had to send them home.

From the OIB to the government, everyone was stunned by Vallerand's position given the engineers hadn't yet completed their evaluation of the damage. It would have been more reasonable to determine whether or not the fall of the infamous beam was an isolated incident before stirring up the public.

The engineers' conclusions came swiftly. The problem was contained to the location where the collapse had occurred and didn't impact the solidity and safety of the stadium as a whole.

But the damage had been done. In the minds of the people, Olympic Stadium was unsafe. Many swore never to set foot in it again.

The remainder of the season became a nightmare. Vallerand's directive meant the team had to play its final 13 home dates on the road. It was quite a headache for National League executives, who had to turn the home schedules of the other teams upside down to fit in those games.

We claimed $3.9 million in compensation from the OIB for revenue lost during the temporary closure of the stadium. But the end of the 1991 season wasn't the only concern. The 1992 season was also at risk. If the stadium didn't reopen in time, the Expos would have to play somewhere other than Montreal. In that case, the league's schedule for the upcoming season would have to be completely revamped.

This element of uncertainty was significant. Professional sports teams plan their travel months in advance to reduce costs and to avoid having the players constantly zigzag across the continent. So the problems at Olympic Stadium affected not only the Expos but also every team in the National League.

To clear up the situation, National League president Bill White arrived in Montreal to meet with OIB president Pierre Bibeau and me. The meeting took place in Bibeau's office.

John Parisella, Premier Robert Bourassa's chief of staff, also attended. After admitting Vallerand had gone too far, Parisella promised White the stadium would be ready for the following season's home opener. Bourassa's chief of staff impressed the National League president. An avid baseball fan, Parisella knew the lineup of the St. Louis Cardinals, during the time White had played for them, by heart. White was also impressed with Parisella's demeanour. At the end of the meeting, he suggested to Parisella that he move to Washington, DC, to replace John Sununu as the White House chief of staff.

White came out of that meeting a little more reassured about the reopening of the stadium, but he remained perplexed about our overall situation. He said to me, "You'll never get out of this, here in Montreal. The time may have come to move the team."

I shook my head. "You're wrong, Bill," I said. "We will succeed. It's a matter of time."

White wasn't at all convinced.

The cancellation of the final 13 home games put an end to a trying season. The ball club posted its lowest attendance since 1976, when it was still at Jarry Park. Only 978,076 people went to Olympic Stadium in 1991, compared with 1,421,388 the previous year—the last year under Charles Bronfman.

On June 22, 1991, soon after the arrival of the new owners, I had revealed to Jeff Blair of the Montreal *Gazette* that we were aiming for 2,000,000 in attendance. Rather a tall order for a wounded stadium.

CHAPTER 7

The Trade

On the field, Buck Rodgers' replacement was taking his first steps as manager. Tom Runnells was competent, enthusiastic, and adored arguing with the umpires, to the great pleasure of the fans. But his inexperience, his lack of maturity, and, mostly, his rigidity eventually hurt him.

With the players, it was a disaster. Runnells' arrival at spring training dressed in military garb and driving an army jeep, to impress his charges and show them who was boss, was hardly a stroke of genius. The players didn't find it the least bit funny. Poor Runnells never recovered.

We had better luck with Dave Dombrowski's replacement, Dan Duquette, an enthusiastic and energetic young wolf who'd also come up through our organization.

After witnessing Runnells' difficulties, Duquette proposed hiring a bench coach after the 1991 season. The new coach would be the manager's associate in the dugout. His name was Felipe Alou. Longtime manager of the Class A Florida State League team in West Palm Beach, Alou had proven himself in the organization. Duquette thought he was ready to play a role in Montreal with the big club.

While the 1991 season had been disappointing in many respects, I could at least count on a competent relief team to help rebuild the club. I hoped to complete this rebuilding in three or four years. If everything went well, if everything went as planned, the Expos would be contenders in 1994 or 1995.

Yet the 1992 season got off to a disastrous start. In the wake of his spring-training "joke," Runnells lost control of the clubhouse. With a sub-.500 record, the team was having a deplorable early season. The situation absolutely had to be straightened out.

"What if we gave the job to Felipe?" Duquette suggested to me as we attempted to find a solution to the ball club's slump.

A native of the Dominican Republic, Alou had been with the organization for more than 16 years. In September 1973, he participated as a player in a pennant drive. After his retirement as a player, he continued his career in the minor leagues as a manager and coach. At the end of the 1970s, Alou worked briefly in Montreal with Dick Williams, then with Bill Virdon and Jim Fanning in 1984. His wife, Lucie Gagnon, was a Montrealer.

There was no doubt Alou was devoted to the organization. But could he manage a ball club in the big leagues? Duquette and I both thought he could. On May 22, 1992, Duquette offered Alou the job.

His reaction was one of concern. Even if Major League Baseball boasted many players from the Dominican Republic, Alou would be the first from that country to manage a big-league team. He would be only the fourth manager from the Caribbean in major-league history. Alou had expected to continue on and finish his career either in the shadow of a manager or perhaps back in the minor leagues. Our offer would put him into the glare of the spotlight, which worried him a little. He well knew that the job of a manager is risky; all it takes is one bad season to suddenly find oneself out of a job. Before getting on board, he wanted to make sure he'd remain in the organization if things didn't work out. Alou doubted his ability to manage the team, and he asked me for additional guarantees.

"Whatever happens, Felipe, you are with the Expos for good," I told him. "I guarantee you that."

He wasn't convinced. To make him feel secure, Duquette and I proposed calling him the interim manager. In our minds, Alou was the new manager of the team, and the job was permanent. But the "interim" label seemed to reassure him.

"It doesn't change a thing for us," I said to Alou. "There is only one manager, and that's you. When you want to change the official title, say the word."

Several years later, in his off-the-record comments to reporters, Alou would say we stuck the "interim" label on him upon his nomination as manager only because he was Latin American. The reality was much different. The incident was a perfect illustration of his personality. Alou never hesitated to rewrite history to serve his personal interests. In addition to being an excellent manager and an exceptional baseball man, he was a master manipulator.

Interim or not, Alou was our new manager. He had all the benefits—and all the responsibilities—of the job. And he wasted no time getting the ball club back on the road to victory. With a 17-20 record and bereft of on-field leadership, the club had been a mere shadow of its former self. Alou's arrival changed all that. Even though the team finished nine games behind the division leaders, it ended the season in second place with a record of 87-75. The .537 winning percentage was the club's best since 1987. It was, in fact, the second-best record since the 1981 season.

Attendance also improved. Olympic Stadium, now officially declared "safe," welcomed 1,731,566 fans to watch the club— nearly twice as many as the previous season, which, it was true, had been cut short by the collapse of the concrete beam.

The rebuilding of the team begun at the 1991 winter meetings was already producing good results. That year we traded first-baseman Andres Galarraga, who was no longer part of our plans, to the St. Louis Cardinals for starting pitcher Ken Hill. The goal of the trade was to improve our pitching situation. We were convinced Hill would be the ace of the starting rotation. At the winter meetings, we also ceded reliever Barry Jones to the Philadelphia Phillies and received catcher Darrin Fletcher in return. And there was more. We traded Dave Martinez, Scott Ruskin, and Willie Greene to the Cincinnati Reds as part of a trade that also involved the Los Angeles Dodgers. The result was that Dodgers reliever John Wetteland ended up in Montreal after a short detour via Cincinnati.

Dan Duquette and Kevin Kennedy were the brains behind this trade. Kennedy, the Expos' director of player development, had grown to appreciate Wetteland and his talents when he was in the Dodgers' organization. He believed the young man was a power pitcher with a brilliant future.

There was no doubt we came out the winners in this three-way deal, as well as in the trades with the Cards and Phillies. The future would bear that out. As well, by trading Galarraga, Martinez, Ruskin, and Greene, we saved $4 million in salaries.

With their flair and tremendous baseball knowledge, Duquette and his team met the challenge in remarkable fashion. They improved the team despite the limited means at their disposal. That was the way it had to be. I was extremely proud of their work.

Unfortunately, it didn't appear to impress the media nearly as much. Most commentators criticized the trades and accused the Expos of trading "our players" for a bunch of unknowns. Wetteland was even given the nickname "John Who?"

Beyond the financial considerations, strictly on a baseball level, we proved we were daring. The basic philosophy of the team would always remain the same. Once the young rookies demonstrated they could play in the big leagues, the veterans were ushered out.

For example, when free-agent shortstop Spike Owen decided to offer his services to another team, we received several picks in the following year's amateur draft in return. To replace Owen, we called on Wilfredo Cordero, who came from one of our minor-league affiliates. The same thing occurred with pitcher Dennis Martinez. Unable to offer him a contract commensurate with his talent, we had to give him up in exchange for a few draft picks. Young, promising players who'd continue their development in our farm system. Along the same lines, even though he was an excellent player and a remarkable clubhouse leader, Tim Wallach left for Los Angeles because we were convinced Sean Berry and Shane Andrews had reached the level of development required to replace him at third base.

The 1993 season was even better than that of 1992. With Alou at the helm and younger, hungrier players on board, the ball club once again finished second in its division. But this time we were only three games behind the leaders. The 94-68 record was the team's best since 1979.

Duquette and I were now convinced we had a fabulous team on our hands. But we weren't standing still—far from it. A few small adjustments were still needed, notably on the mound, where we'd been weakened by the departure of Martinez.

On November 19, 1993, Duquette hit one out of the park. He sent second-baseman Delino DeShields to the Los Angeles Dodgers for young right-handed pitcher Pedro Martinez. Duquette was convinced Mike Lansing could do just as well, if not better, than DeShields at second base.

The reporters cried foul. Michael Farber of the Montreal *Gazette* led the charge: "Deal is rotten to the core. Expos' one big deal to balance books will sicken fans," he wrote. He continued on, ridiculing the following year's starting lineup: ". . . You have a sublime prospect at first base (Cliff Floyd) who has proven absolutely nothing at the big-league level, a poor man's Bret Barberie with better speed at second (Mike Lansing), an inconsistent but improving shortstop going into just his second full season (Wil Cordero) and a hard-working third baseman who has some speed and some pop but who probably is a better player off the bench (Sean Berry)." A disaster, Farber concluded. His colleague, Pat Hickey, added this: "There's no puzzle why the Expos made the deal. Too many decisions are made to balance the books."

Same uproar on the francophone side. "For a matter of money, the Expos sacrificed Delino DeShields and obtained Pedro Martinez," wrote Serge Touchette of the *Journal de Montréal*. Same thing at *La Presse*: "Money, the Expos' only concern," wrote Pierre Ladouceur. "Trading Delino DeShields to the Los Angeles Dodgers shows, once again, that the Expos executives are thinking only about reducing their payroll." Ladouceur's colleague Philippe Cantin added this: "So begins the fire sale; where will it end?"

On vacation in Florida, I participated in a conference call with the media to calm everyone. I was accused on all fronts of having betrayed the fans, of having dismantled the successful 1993 squad. I tried to set the record straight, but no one wanted to hear it. Everyone had one thing in mind: the money. One reporter even went so far as to declare, jokingly, that the Expos had acquired Pedro Martinez to replace Dennis Martinez only because he could use his predecessor's jersey and save the team the extra expense.

The reporters were partially right. As in the deal that brought John Wetteland to Montreal, the acquisition of Pedro Martinez did significantly reduce our payroll. DeShields' salary had been $1,537,500 the previous season, while Martinez had made just $114,000, slightly above the major-league minimum at the time. Those numbers prevented the media from evaluating the trade on its own merits. They simply couldn't comprehend the team had also improved on the field.

Not everyone thought that way. As recently as August 2001, on the U.S. sports network ESPN, renowned baseball expert Peter Gammons declared the trade that sent DeShields to Los Angeles and brought Martinez to Montreal to be the fourth-greatest trade in baseball history. Not bad for a "fire sale."

Despite the media's acerbic criticism, which obviously had repercussions on fan morale, we approached the 1994 season with a lot of confidence. After the trade, Duquette said to me, "Claude, this year we're going to win." For the first time in our team's history, we could go the distance.

Unfortunately, the fans were slow to get on board. Season-ticket sales declined for the 1994 season despite the team's excellent performance the preceding year. Every year it seemed as though we had to work twice as hard to convince the fans of their team's value.

Duquette was right. As the summer heated up, it became more and more apparent we were the club to beat. Fans couldn't believe what they were seeing. The dismantling everyone had feared didn't occur—just the opposite. The group of players appearing nightly at Olympic Stadium was the finest baseball team Montreal had ever known, without a doubt the best team in baseball in 1994—in either league.

At first, many thought the ball club would crumble sooner or later, just as pitcher Mark Langston had in 1989. But game after game, in Montreal or on the road, the Expos put up one remarkable performance after another. Duquette's "adjustments" were paying off. The arrival of Wetteland, Hill, Martinez, and the other players had transformed the team.

We were in second place at the end of April. But we didn't remain there long. In July, we took over the division lead with a six-game cushion over our closest rivals, the Atlanta Braves. In the middle of August, we were 74-40, an impressive winning percentage of .649, and we still led the second-place Braves by six games.

It was the team's best record since its arrival in the National League in 1969. This year's model might even have been better than the teams at the end of the 1970s and beginning of the 1980s, when the Expos won the division title. And fans were returning to Olympic Stadium in droves. Our dream—the dream shared by Duquette, our entire team, and me—was within our grasp. The World Series might be held in Montreal. . . .

Then came a rude awakening.

On August 12, the Players Association went on strike, which lasted for months. The rest of the season's games were cancelled. For only the second time in the history of Major League Baseball, there would be no World Series.

CHAPTER 8

Painful Days Ahead

People often need to point to a specific moment or event to find a simple cause for a complex problem. For many fans, the Expos' misfortunes boiled down to two seminal moments: Blue Monday, in October 1981, when the club was eliminated from the National League Championship Series against the Los Angeles Dodgers by a Rick Monday home run in the top of the ninth inning at Olympic Stadium, and August 12, 1994, when the players went on strike.

The strike had been in the air for several months as we were heading toward the championship. We all hoped the Players Association wouldn't carry out its threat. But as the weeks passed, it became obvious we were headed toward an impasse. The major issue was salaries. The owners wanted to keep them down; the players obviously opposed any form of salary cap and were determined to make their point.

We weren't much affected by the question of a salary cap. Whether it was accepted by the players or not, we'd never have the means to pay high salaries. What concerned us more was the implementation of a revenue-sharing system.

I participated in the committees that approved the new system. But I didn't take part in either the Labour Relations Committee or the Negotiating Committee as such. I didn't play the predominant role in those debates many alleged later on. I was even accused of purposely turning the players against us to push them to strike. On the other hand, during the course of the negotiations, I ratified the initiatives and recommendations of my colleagues. Like the other team owners, I stood behind the group even though I hadn't contributed to the formation of its strategy.

The strategy itself was a failure. Pushing the players too far solved nothing; the intensification of the conflict led directly to a strike. Still, we were surprised by the Players Association's decision. I'd never imagined it would come to a strike. Everyone, the players included, believed the work stoppage would be short. Unfortunately, it dragged on for eight long months. The U.S. Federal Court finally decreed the reopening of training camps in May 1995. The owners were forced to give in to the players on every level.

From then on, salaries began to spiral out of control. But the impact of the work stoppage took an even greater toll on the fans. The image of Major League Baseball was tarnished by the strike.

The strike only aggravated my relations with some of the members of the consortium, particularly Jocelyn Proteau of Desjardins. Since acquiring the team, Proteau and I had crossed swords on numerous occasions. Proteau, like Jacques Ménard and Mark Routtenberg, adored being in the spotlight. He wanted us to invite the media to partnership meetings to update them about the group's positions on the major issues of the day. Conscious of Desjardins' corporate image, Proteau wanted to associate his company with the Expos' good moves—not a good idea but understandable.

More difficult to comprehend were his attempts to interfere in the team's internal affairs. One day Proteau took me aside and asked me to get rid of Richard Morency, the team's vice president of marketing and communications.

"That's out of the question," I said. "Richard and his team are doing a fantastic job."

Morency wasn't Proteau's only target. Proteau complained incessantly; he never agreed with me about anything.

At that point, we continued to have a serious cash-flow problem. At the end of each season, Major League Baseball's Central Fund redistributed to each team, in equal measure, the revenue derived from the highly rated broadcasts of the World Series and the all-star game on the U.S. television networks. So even though we'd never participated in the World Series, we still received several million dollars a year, as we had since the first year of the team's existence. The potential cancellation of the 1994 postseason could force us to kiss millions of dollars good-bye.

Given their other sources of revenue, the major-market teams could quickly correct the situation the following year. In Montreal, that was impossible. When a team makes a lot of money, all it has to do is tighten the belt a little, reduce the payroll a little, and the losses are quickly erased. But we had no breathing room. Every dollar was essential to our survival.

In short, we needed a helping hand from Desjardins, a line of credit that would allow us to survive the labour conflict. Ménard and I headed to Proteau's office to discuss the matter. The discussion didn't last long. Proteau was unequivocal: if there was a strike, he wouldn't finance the ball club. His position seemed completely irrational to me. The Expos were worth $150 million; the team's debt was barely $10 million. Any banker would have agreed to bail us out for a few months. Any banker, it seemed, except Proteau. Having had to award exclusivity for our financial services to Desjardins, we couldn't turn to the Bank of Montreal, for example, to get a short-term loan or a line of credit. Had Proteau wanted to push us into bankruptcy, he couldn't have done a better job.

Back in my office, I got on the phone to New York and spoke to Jeff White, Major League Baseball's vice president of finance. I was just in time. White was literally—within the next few minutes—about to complete interim financing for several teams with an American banking syndicate, a group of banks ready to provide lines of credit to professional baseball teams. As collateral, the banks simply took future national television broadcast revenues. I hopped on board and, at the same time, sent Proteau and his precious "exclusivity" packing. Thanks to Major League Baseball's banking services, we obtained a $50 million Canadian line of credit that saw us through the strike.

Not surprisingly, the employees were demoralized in the spring of 1995. Everyone had worked so hard, at every level, and the result had been a season that had simply fizzled out. I did my best to encourage my staff, but I could clearly see they were down.

When the season started up in May, I had to face yet another worrisome financial situation. During the strike, the club had continued to pay operating costs such as the salaries of employees, scouts, and minor-league players, thanks to the line of credit obtained from the United States. But the situation was hardly resolved for the upcoming season. The cancellation of the World Series had cost us close to $16 million Canadian. The three previous years, thanks to tight management, we'd ended each fiscal year with a slight profit. Now the situation was quite different.

The first solution, used by other teams dealing with the same problem, consisted of asking the owners to cover the teams' losses. In the Charles Bronfman era, that was the usual escape route. But even Bronfman would likely have balked at absorbing such a substantial loss. During the 22 years he ran the team, his accumulated deficit added up to only $44 million.

The situation was more dire than it had ever been. And it was out of the question for me to approach my partners. I knew very well they wouldn't want to put another dime into the club. I didn't even have to ask them.

So I had one option remaining: cut payroll, and therefore dismantle our winning team, and rebuild it with young players from our farm system. Had I kept all the players from the 1994 team, we would have lost $25 million in 1995, which would have increased our accumulated losses to $40 million in all. The club, quite simply, would have been flirting with bankruptcy.

A fire sale. This time I used that expression myself. In April 1995, I gave Kevin Malone, the former scouting director who'd replaced Dan Duquette as general manager, the order to start making trades. Dead inside, we went at it systematically. The three highest-paid players on the team (Ken Hill, Marquis Grissom, and John Wetteland) were traded. Larry Walker became a free agent. We didn't make him an offer, which allowed us to receive two picks in the following year's amateur draft in return. I personally negotiated with George Steinbrenner, the colourful owner of the New York Yankees, who acquired Wetteland for outfield/first-base prospect Fernando Seguignol and the sum of $2 million, payable in four instalments of $500,000.

The members of the consortium witnessed the dismantling of the team without really knowing how to react. But the fire sale raised questions from Mark Routtenberg, who criticized me for giving up two players too many. "It wouldn't have changed anything," I told him. "What's the difference between a $15 million deficit and a $25 million deficit? Either way we wouldn't have made it."

The reaction from the media wasn't as negative as we'd expected. *La Presse* columnist Réjean Tremblay even approved of my decision. Given the Expos' financial situation, he wrote, the trades had to be evaluated with the head and not the heart. "The strike happened, and there's no point in crying about it," he wrote. "The first impulse is to criticize Expos' management. We all want to dream and gamble with other people's money."

Tremblay added that he, just like the fans, would have liked us to go for broke and try to win it all by keeping last year's team intact. But there was no guarantee we'd win the championship even if we kept the same players. "That's the heart and the gut talking, not the head," Tremblay wrote. "Common sense says baseball fans don't seem to like baseball as much as they love winning. Common sense says Claude Brochu did the right thing in selling his players and gambling on the eternal rebuilding of Nos Z'Amours. There was nothing else to do."

Later in his column, Tremblay blamed the tepidity of the fans in the face of the team's limited budget: "Montreal is a great major-league city; it is the fans that are minor-league. That's the truth, and if I were Claude Brochu—if it were my money and the money of my financial partners on the table, I would do as he did."

George Steinbrenner agreed. When the trade was announced, Steinbrenner told American reporters he couldn't understand why

Montreal fans didn't support the Expos' organization. In 20 years, Steinbrenner said, he hadn't seen a better job done by a manager (Felipe Alou) and a president (me). And he added, "The Expos had the best record in baseball despite the second-smallest payroll in the majors. If the fans don't care, they don't deserve to keep their team."

But why didn't the baseball fans care? What was missing between the fans and the team? On several occasions, our marketing initiatives were blamed—often wrongly—for Quebecers' lukewarm interest in their baseball team. We had commissioned a number of studies over the years in an attempt to better understand and better reach the people of Quebec.

The majority of men (60%), spanning all age groups and social classes, liked baseball. Many were diehard fans. Others were casual fans who came to the stadium occasionally to have fun and relax. Interestingly, several surveys in the early 1990s revealed fans to be satisfied with the advertising and promotional campaigns. In fact, it was not the marketing efforts that sparked their interest in the Expos but the entertainment value, the motivation and team spirit of the players, as well as their harmonious relationship with management. Most people said they were satisfied with the work accomplished by the club, yet they continued to stay away from home games. They said they liked baseball but, in the same breath, affirmed they weren't interested in actually coming to games.

Quite the paradox.

In 1994, we tried to dig deeper. New surveys revealed that the progressive disaffection of Montrealers stemmed from three principal factors: first, the fans found the tickets too expensive; second, they judged the stadium inadequate for baseball; and third, many of them preferred to follow the team on television or radio. Once again none of these responses blamed the team's marketing programs.

On the corporate side, the reactions echoed those of the fans. Corporate executives thought the stadium poorly located, the ambience gloomy and boring, and the services offered limited. They also thought 81 home games were far too many. The result was that the corporate boxes were emptying out at the same rate as the rest of the stadium. Individuals and companies weren't as passionate as they had been, as captivated as they once had been at the idea of attending an Expos game—even if the team was performing well on the field.

Another characteristic of the local fan base made our job particularly difficult. According to several surveys, Montreal consumers attending concerts, shows, or sporting events didn't like to buy tickets in advance—unless those tickets were very difficult to get. They decided to go somewhere on the spur of the moment and expected there would be room. We had to deal with an impulsive public, which wasn't the case in the rest of North America.

On some days, only a few hundred fans appeared at the ticket windows. On other occasions, no fewer than 20,000 people suddenly decided to attend a game. On average, three of four fans chose to attend a baseball game on a whim. According to the surveys, 52% of fans decided to attend on the day of the game. Another 22% decided to attend a game between one and three days before it.

Elsewhere, if the local team goes through a difficult period, the tickets sold are still used. In Montreal, everyone stays at home.

In this context, Morency and his marketing team had to work twice as hard and show plenty of imagination to try to attract fans to the stadium. Pregame baseball clinics for youngsters, special ticket promotions, the presence of our players on Saturdays in various city parks, the kids' opening day, and even dollar hot dogs! Not to mention the formidable Youppi, very popular with the young fans even if baseball purists accused the team's mascot of preventing them from enjoying the beauty of the game.

We always had to take the divergent interests of the fans into account. Some loved the stadium entertainment; others didn't want to hear anything about it. The giant screen got on some fans' nerves, others thought the music was too loud or not loud enough, and so on. We attempted the impossible in trying to please everyone.

Despite all these efforts, the message never got through. We could have been tempted to shift the blame onto the media, whose negative coverage during those years might have fed the fans' disaffection. In addition, several reporters complained of tensions with some media-relations employees. They also bemoaned the lack of openness from management.

Today I regret not having shared more information with reporters. I regret not having tried to integrate them more fully into our various projects.

CHAPTER 9

Selling the Team?

The Expos finished fifth in the division in 1995, 24 games behind the leaders. With a record of 66-78, a winning percentage of .458, it was our worst season since 1991. We'd limited the financial losses with the departure of Walker, Wetteland, Grissom, and Hill. And the new television-rights agreement allowed us to breathe a little more easily. But the long, useless, and costly strike and the dismantling of the 1994 championship team added to the other problems and made the task of "selling" the team to the fans increasingly complicated.

Yet we were hardly a "lemon," as the media seemed to think. They often described the Expos as a Triple-A team incapable of keeping its best players. With the exception of 1995, though, the Expos had always put together a remarkable record. In 1996, despite the loss of several key players the previous year, we finished second in our division with 88 wins and 74 losses, a very respectable .543 winning percentage. Not bad for a Triple-A team.

From 1991 to 1996, we ranked third in all of Major League Baseball in wins, behind only the Atlanta Braves and the Chicago White Sox. On two occasions, we finished second in our division, and in 1994, when the strike hit, we were the best team in baseball.

The management of the franchise was equally remarkable; there were only two deficit years during that period. In 1994, we had to absorb a $16 million loss in the wake of the strike. In 1996, another loss, in the order of $7 million. In 1991, 1992, 1993, and

1995, on the other hand, we ended each fiscal year with a slight profit.

The company was viable, but its margin for error was ever decreasing. The public's disaffection really hurt the team. Elsewhere in baseball, season-ticket sales increased in 1995 and 1996; the opposite occurred in Montreal. The fan base, both individuals and corporations, continued to erode, while in most of the other baseball cities people were getting their taste back for the sport after the difficult strike period.

The fact was that, since 1989, the team's revenues had stagnated. That year our payroll was $18 million U.S., slightly above the major-league average. In 1997, the payroll was $22 million U.S., barely half the overall average of $43 million U.S.

On the television side, it was the same story. In the other Major League Baseball cities, revenues from television broadcast rights averaged $12 million U.S. In Montreal, we received just $2 million. Even the eight American franchises operating in small markets could still count on an average of $4 million for television rights, double what we received.

From 1991 to 1996, we tried everything to find new sources of revenue. My initiative regarding the changes to the National League Television Agreement went toward that end. On the management side, we tried to maximize revenue from food concessions and parking. We worked hard to stimulate advertising and corporate suite sales. From 1992 to 1997, revenues in that area increased 250%.

Despite all the efforts, our revenues were barely half the major-league average. We'd managed to keep our heads above water throughout those years, but I was more than aware that the current we were swimming against was getting stronger and stronger. How could we get out of this precarious situation?

At my request, Executive Vice President of Business Development Laurier Carpentier and Vice President of Finance Michel Bussière prepared two potential scenarios to be submitted to the other consortium partners. They were, in fact, financial projections for the next five years.

The first scenario was both proactive and aggressive. It was the scenario everyone wished for. We were told that, if we increased the payroll, the fans would come and see the Expos play.

The projection provided for an across-the-board increase in the team's revenues and expenses. The payroll would increase from $19.5 million U.S. to $32 million U.S., the industry average in 1996; annual attendance would increase to 2.2 million (from 1.6 million in 1996). This forecast also factored in an increase in the amount received by the club from Major League Baseball's revenue-sharing program, from $6 million to $10 million a year.

According to this hypothesis, the ball club would lose $64 million over that five-year period. In other words, even if we put more money into the club and attracted more fans, we'd continue to lose an average of nearly $13 million annually.

The other projection was based on tight fiscal management, the same philosophy we'd favoured for the past several years. It was, in effect, the survival strategy. According to the forecasts, both revenues and expenses would decline. The payroll would remain the same as in 1996, $16 million U.S.—half what the other teams were paying. We forecast that attendance would drop to 1.1 million fans a year. Conversely, we expected revenue-sharing money to increase from $7 million to $15 million a year. Under this scenario, our losses would total $15 million between 1996 and 2001, some $3 million a year.

Regardless of the evolution of baseball in Montreal over the next few years, and even if we maintained the status quo, the team would lose money. It seemed to be apparent we were headed toward financial disaster. Our situation was hardly unique. With player salaries having practically doubled between 1990 and 1993, 24 of the 28 major-league baseball teams had posted losses during those years.

The analysis completed by Carpentier, Bussière, and the specialists they consulted identified Olympic Stadium as one of the key elements in their projections. Their hypotheses took for granted that the Expos and Olympic Stadium were inseparable, that we would always play there.

That infamous stadium was becoming more and more reviled, especially by the fans; surveys we commissioned over the years confirmed it. The venue was poorly designed for baseball, people didn't feel comfortable there, and the multiple problems related to the roof and the structure had confirmed the public's apprehensions. Since becoming president of the team, I'd gotten the Olympic Installations Board to make some major modifications to accommodate us, such as the installation of a giant screen. But it wasn't enough.

But what if we owned the stadium? In exchange for acquiring Olympic Stadium for the symbolic sum of one dollar, for example, we'd assume responsibility for operations, except obviously for capital expenditures related to repairs and maintenance. Could we then generate sufficient incremental revenues to make survival possible? We were certain of one thing; the government would welcome our taking this political hot potato out of its hands.

In 1995, I commissioned a study on the subject from a group of expert consultants led by Jean Corbeil, the former mayor of Ville d'Anjou and a former labour minister in the Brian Mulroney government. Also participating was Richard Le Lay, who'd soon become my principal advisor with the Quebec government, as well as representatives from the accounting firm of Price Waterhouse; the law firm of Martineau, Walker; and A. Denault Construction. Members of this group had made major contributions to the success of the privatization of Dorval and Mirabel airports.

The experts' conclusions were clear. The particularities of the facility imposed constraints that were both unacceptable and insurmountable. Its extravagant dimensions, its sombre and cavernous interior, the layout of its corporate boxes and seats all served to limit its usability. As well, the stadium was dilapidated; maintaining it would require major investments in the coming years. Yes, revenues could be increased, but not to a level that would allow the team to compete. In the experts' opinion, the risk was too great; we were better off not jumping aboard a sinking ship.

Corbeil was the only one not to share the opinion submitted by the group he led. Despite the arguments advanced by the specialists, Corbeil continued to believe in the privatization of the stadium and, eventually, of the entire Olympic Park complex. His position could be explained by the fact that he was very involved in the development of the eastern part of the island, where the stadium was located. When he was the minister responsible for the Montreal region, Corbeil had tried to convince the Montreal Canadiens to build their new arena there to stimulate economic growth in that sector of the city.

The two of us discussed it on several occasions, but Corbeil refused to admit the obvious. Despite the conclusions drawn by the experts, he remained convinced that, with the help and encouragement of the City of Montreal, the Expos could become profitable if they remained at Olympic Stadium.

The Expos weren't the only team to have a complex and frustrating relationship with the facility in which they played and welcomed their fans. Across North America, because of the increases in expenses engendered by ever-increasing payrolls, several teams chose to move into smaller, more central venues, specifically built for baseball, in which they could achieve a maximum return on each home game.

The strike setback and the inability of Major League Baseball to impose a ceiling on the players' salary demands only served to accelerate the movement. Owners had to find supplementary sources of revenue. They believed the large stadiums built in the 1960s and 1970s, such as the Astrodome in Houston, the Kingdome in Seattle, and the Metrodome in Minneapolis couldn't generate sufficient revenue and no longer corresponded to what baseball fans were looking for.

It wasn't the first time the industry had to adapt. At the beginning of the 20th century, when baseball became the most popular sport in America and ticket sales constituted the main source of revenue for team owners, they began building bigger venues to allow the largest possible number of fans to attend games. Erected during this period were memorable stadiums such as Pittsburgh's

Forbes Field, Philadelphia's Shibe Park, and, most of all, Chicago's Wrigley Field.

In the 1960s, a different trend emerged. Fans were demanding more in terms of comfort and accessibility, and baseball was catching up in terms of technology. Unless major renovations were made, such as at Yankee Stadium in New York, the old stadiums no longer suited the needs of most teams. More versatile ones were built and equipped with artificial playing surfaces, which could host not only baseball games but also football games, rock concerts, and even trade shows. Toronto's SkyDome, with its retractable roof, hotel complex, restaurants, and office space, marked the apogee of that type of construction.

Unfortunately, those huge, very costly buildings no longer corresponded to baseball's economy at the end of the century. By the time we were considering leaving Olympic Stadium, several American teams had already made a similar leap. The Chicago White Sox, Baltimore Orioles, Cleveland Indians, Atlanta Braves, Colorado Rockies, and Texas Rangers had moved into new stadiums designed with a radically different approach in mind.

These "renaissance" stadiums revived the atmosphere of the old ballparks while taking advantage of modern technology. Designed exclusively for baseball, with old-time natural-grass surfaces, these ballparks, as they were now being referred to, were the height of modern comfort. They also met the emerging demands of the modern consumer. As we have seen in the movie industry, where large, single-screen theatres have given way to multiplexes offering several types of entertainment, fans attending games at the new ballparks enjoyed a multitude of services: major restaurants, games areas, fashion boutiques, and more. In Baltimore, people would head to Camden Yards in the afternoon to take advantage of all the services found there, even though the game itself wouldn't begin until evening. Jacobs Field in Cleveland and Coors Field in Denver became "in" places, hot spots where the main attraction wasn't only baseball. As well, city administrations discovered these ballparks could bring major economic returns in addition to sparking the revitalization of the downtown areas in which they were located.

But the team owners were really the big winners in this game. They quickly realized these new facilities were much more profitable than the immense stadiums of the past. As in Montreal, the cities of Baltimore and Cleveland had gone through hard times in terms of attendance and season-ticket sales. The new stadiums allowed them to correct the situation. Teams that had lost money between 1990 and 1993 were now profitable.

Within the partnership, the atmosphere was growing onerous.

For me, the arrival of Pierre Michaud to represent Provigo within the consortium hadn't been a good thing. He immediately joined the ranks of the "frustrated," as I referred to that group. I could see Michaud didn't believe in the Expos' future in Montreal. According to him, the business community was in no way interested in the success of the team. Soon Michaud offered Provigo's shares to anyone who wanted to buy them, even at a discount. No one came forward, so he remained in the partnership. And he wasn't particularly happy about it.

During one meeting, Michaud called for a major change in the role of the partnership committee. He suggested the committee function as a regular board of directors, with full powers. That would have amounted to dismantling the limited partnership and replacing it with a new partnership, which would have significantly decreased my authority as general partner. I believed he was appointing himself spokesman for the group of dissatisfied partners by putting that idea forward. Knowing full well Major League Baseball would never accept such a change, and not wanting to entrust the Expos to someone who didn't believe in the team, I rejected the proposal. Michaud was furious. At the end of the meeting, he turned to me and said, "You want to run this alone? You are going to be and feel very alone."

The idea of increasing the consortium's powers, of exerting more control over me, became Michaud's main preoccupation from that moment on. After that, every time journalists quoted an "unnamed source," they were quoting Michaud. He was the one revealing the problems related to the management of the consortium and the control of the team to the media.

In the months that followed, the climate gradually deteriorated, and my support began to crumble. Whatever happened, I had to battle Proteau, Blanchet, Roberge, and now Michaud, who tried by every means possible to limit my authority and thwart my initiatives.

During our wrangles with Revenu-Québec, I realized once again to what extent several members of the consortium were putting their personal or corporate interests ahead of those of the ball club. We'd been at odds with the province's ministry of revenue since 1986. The issue was the players' contribution to the provincial health-insurance plan.

This program was financed by the imposition of a tax representing 4.26% of a company's payroll. Given that most of the team's players, coaches, and trainers didn't live in Canada, the Régie de l'assurance-maladie du Québec (RAMQ) deducted this tax only on the portion of their salaries earned in Quebec, the home games. Consequently, the tax to be paid by the Expos was assessed on only 41% of the ball club's payroll, as was the case with player income taxes. Both Ottawa and Quebec had accepted this percentage from the beginning.

We'd operated on this basis since 1979—with the RAMQ's approval, of course. In 1986, though, Revenu-Québec changed its mind and claimed our contributions should be calculated on the entire payroll—and that this calculation should be retroactive to January 1, 1982. According to the ministry's calculations, the contributions, interest, and penalties we owed to the government added up to about $12 million. A financial catastrophe.

For nine years, we contested this decision and tried to make all the ministers directly or indirectly associated with the issue aware of it, to no avail. Even the premier's office refused to get involved. We had only one recourse: the courts. We hired two excellent lawyers, Guy Dupont and Francois Barette of the firm of Phillips & Vineberg, to appeal Revenu-Québec's decision. On August 9, 1995, the Quebec Superior Court ruled in our favour.

But the war was far from over. Pursuant to the judge's decision, Revenu-Québec modified the health-insurance law to be able, in the future, to impose RAMQ contributions on the entire payroll of the ball club.

I refused to give up. I told the partners I intended to move the team's payroll services to West Palm Beach, Florida, to escape Revenu-Québec harassment and protect the partnership. I also suggested we move the team's minor-league administration offices to Florida since the minor-league operations were already in the United States. And I asked our lawyers to initiate legal proceedings against Revenu-Québec to recover a portion of our $1 million legal bill; we were successful there as well.

The partners were furious, particularly Jocelyn Proteau and Claude Blanchet. "This means job losses for Quebecers," said Proteau, appalled.

"Unfortunately," I replied. "But there is no other solution."

I understood the position of both Desjardins and the Solidarity Fund. The two partners were concerned about corporate image. What would the public say if these two Quebec-based institutions allowed jobs in a company they owned to be transferred out of province? They were prepared to do whatever it took to preserve their reputations, even if it cost the ball club millions.

"Not to mention," another partner added, "that it's not a good idea to get Revenu-Québec on our backs."

"Very well. But how are we going to pay these additional taxes?" I asked.

"The important thing is to save jobs in Quebec," insisted Proteau.

I let them talk; in any case, I intended to go ahead. I had the support of my management team, and I knew I was right. The issue went around the table, and all of the co-owners disagreed with me. All of them, without exception. I ignored their opinion. "I have to think of the team, first and foremost," I told them. "Moving the payroll service is a good business decision, and I am going to stand by it. End of discussion."

You could have heard a pin drop. But not for long. Furious, the partners slammed their briefcases shut and left the room. To say the least, I wasn't a popular man that day.

How noble it was that the growth of the Quebec labour force was so near and dear to their hearts. But how many employees, exactly, would lose their jobs as a result of my decision? Three. Those employees would be transferred to West Palm Beach to train the American staff that would replace them. Not nearly enough to warrant such a scene. All of it was complaining for complaining's sake. I knew very well they'd have done exactly as I'd done had they been confronted with the same situation in their own companies.

In September 1996, I outlined the club's precarious financial situation to these "frustrated" partners. While the Corbeil group continued its work, I endeavoured to make the members of the consortium aware of the trends and developments in the industry— notably the new wave of baseball parks. I provided them with an accurate assessment of our situation. Despite the team's recovery from a disappointing 1995 season, and even though we were second in the division (which bode well for a tight, exciting pennant race), attendance had dropped considerably. We expected 300,000 fewer fans at the stadium than we'd planned for in our preseason forecasts, and this drop represented an additional loss of about $4.5 million.

When they heard the numbers, the partners were very concerned. As investors preoccupied mostly with safeguarding their initial investments, the bleak picture I was painting worried them.

The Solidarity Fund's Claude Blanchet called the marketing strategy established at the beginning of the year into question. But it seemed the problem was far more comprehensive than a simple matter of marketing. Our critical condition couldn't be healed by an advertising campaign, no matter how effective.

I briefed the partners on the initiatives undertaken by American owners, also dealing with budgetary restrictions, who'd chosen to build stadiums better attuned to the demands of the fans. I also told them about the growth in revenues resulting from these new ballparks. In Baltimore, for example, season-ticket sales doubled to 27,000. More than 3.7 million fans came to cheer on the Orioles—nearly double the previous year's attendance. The same renaissance occurred in Cleveland. Season-ticket sales tripled to 20,000, and attendance jumped to 3.2 million—also double what it had been in the Indians' old facility, nicknamed "Mistake by the Lake."

The numbers spoke for themselves, but the members of the consortium remained unmoved. For most of them, the construction of a new stadium was premature. Jocelyn Proteau believed a new facility might improve the team's financial situation and avoid the potential $64 million in losses outlined in the report from our management team, but he was far from convinced. According to him, the results reaped by the American owners weren't necessarily applicable to Montreal. Proteau had only one motivation: protecting his $7 million investment. He didn't want to hear about any project that might require him to increase his stake in the team.

Mark Routtenberg went further. Given that the public wasn't reacting favourably to either the marketing campaigns or the fact the team was one of the best in the National League, it wasn't relevant to think about building a new stadium, he thought. Instead, Routtenberg suggested selling the team.

Avie Bennett and Pierre Michaud agreed with him. According to them, we should have prepared plan B: moving the team to the United States. That, of course, directly contradicted what they would say later on.

Jacques Ménard proposed we table the issue until later. Even if the club were to be sold, the team would still play in Montreal in 1997 and probably in 1998, given that Major League Baseball had to be informed at least a year in advance of any potential sale. But waiting wouldn't solve anything. Year after year, the losses would increase, making the situation more and more untenable. We had to act quickly.

Yet no one would budge. I asked my partners to make a business decision, but they were either incapable of making it or refused to make the commitment—perhaps because, for some, their initial investments were made almost on a charitable basis. Emotion or duty drove their initial decision to invest, not running this club as a proper business.

At the next meeting, in November, the co-owners' song remained the same. Claude Blanchet once again attributed the problem to poor marketing. If the team was attracting fewer and fewer fans, he believed, it was because maximum effort hadn't been made to promote the team among fans and corporations.

"Brochu is right," Jim McCoubrey of Télémédia said. "There may not be enough interest in Montreal for a baseball team."

"At Olympic Stadium, that's obvious," I replied. "But if we moved downtown. . . ."

Around the table, opinions varied. It seemed to me that McCoubrey, Jocelyn Proteau of Desjardins, Avie Bennett of McClelland & Stewart, Pierre Michaud of Provigo, Mark Routtenberg of Freemark Investments, and Paul Roberge of Boutiques San Francisco were agreed to put the club up for sale immediately. Jacques Ménard, as well as Louis Tanguay of Bell and Alain Lemaire of Cascades, were still hesitant, but the prospect of selling seemed to appeal to them.

Only Claude Blanchet of the Solidarity Fund still believed the team could survive at Olympic Stadium. "Temporary problems, all of that. All you have to do is to improve your marketing strategies, and the fans will come back to the stadium," he said. Blanchet completely dismissed the data contained in the report prepared by my management team. A seven-year trend is hardly a short-lived phenomenon.

Blanchet and the Solidarity Fund had found themselves in the same situation with the Quebec Nordiques. A co-owner of the team, they had to be resigned to participating in the sale of the club, a sale conducted amid full-blown controversy. They had to explain themselves, justify their actions. The fund was accused of "selling out" a Quebec institution. It is possible Blanchet didn't want to find himself in the same situation with the Expos.

At any rate, his perception of the facts was erroneous. As a graduate in history, I thought reducing our problems to minor marketing issues was like saying World War II was initiated by Germany because of a few border skirmishes with Poland—a rather simplistic view.

Only one of the consortium members supported the solution I'd put forth to move the team to a new downtown stadium. Bill Stinson of Canadian Pacific believed the option was interesting enough, and promising enough, to study in depth.

During subsequent meetings, some of the partners suggested setting up a committee to try to find solutions to the financial impasse in which we found ourselves. This committee, whose mandate was to work jointly with me and advise me if necessary, was made up of Jacques Ménard, Claude Blanchet, Jocelyn Proteau, and Mark Routtenberg, who were joined by Monic Houde of Bell Canada.

Two months later, after one meeting, the committee brought back its conclusions. There weren't many concrete answers; it was obviously easier to debate a problem than to find solutions to it. There was a lot of talk, some sensible observations, but little of substance. The members of the "advisory" committee had to admit they were overwhelmed by the events. They would never meet again.

CHAPTER 10

The Canadiens and the Alouettes

Bob Wetenhall, the American owner of the Montreal Alouettes of the Canadian Football League, loves U2. And his love has nothing to do with the words or music of Bono, the leader of the Irish rock group. In fact, Wetenhall had absolutely no interest in U2 before learning that their show at Olympic Stadium conflicted with an Alouettes playoff game. Wetenhall had to find an alternative. At the last minute, he turned to McGill University's Percival Molson Stadium.

The rest is history. A team that had been piling up losses—$4 million in one year alone—found its way back to quasi-profitability. The move downtown saved the Alouettes from certain death at Olympic Stadium.

In 1993, I was trying by every means possible to find ways to improve our situation. I was looking to maximize the use of our resources, our own personnel, as well as the Olympic Stadium's resources. When Larry Smith, CFL commissioner at the time, came to Montreal, he'd try to convince me to bring back the Alouettes, who'd folded a few years before. It was a project Larry cared a great deal about.

Smith is a good friend of mine. I liked him as a CFL player, as commissioner, and as president of the Alouettes before he was named publisher of the Montreal *Gazette* early in 2002. His reasoning for reviving football in Montreal was based on several indisputable criteria. First and foremost, there was the sport's long tradition in the city: the Alouettes had enjoyed their glory days, and Smith himself had won a Grey Cup in an Alouettes uniform. Second, the province of Quebec supplied the largest number of players to the CFL. Third, there was also the certainty that Montreal would never be awarded a National Football League franchise—local market conditions and financial capacity would never allow it. Those elements, along with the expertise in the world of professional sport the Expos had acquired over the years, convinced Smith he could be successful in his quest.

Montreal needed a football team; that much was obvious. Smith and I had discussed it on many occasions, analysing all the risks involved in such a gamble within the context of Montreal's sports climate: potential gate revenue, per capita expenditures at the concession and souvenir stands, revenue generated by sponsorship and advertising. We'd also examined in detail all the costs of football operations: marketing, public relations, sales, financing and administration, and activities related to the stadium and ticket sales.

We concluded that, to be viable, the ball club would have to attract between 22,000 and 25,000 fans a game at an average cost of $21 per ticket. Drawing on the studies produced by Jean-Marc Léger, we concluded the Expos and Alouettes would benefit from sharing the same management. Marketing, sponsorship sales, financial and administrative services, as well as activities related to Olympic Stadium and ticket sales could be under the same umbrella.

I remained very concerned about the real interest football fans had in going to Olympic Stadium. Taking into account the recent past of the Alouettes, the Concordes (run by Charles Bronfman and Imasco), and the Machine, I was convinced only sustained efforts would recapture the hearts of the fans and rebuild a solid fan base. On the other hand, the Canadian Football League was showing signs of life, of increased stability.

I raised the question with my partners during a meeting of the consortium. But, of course, no one showed any interest. With reason, probably. I hadn't yet understood to what extent Olympic Stadium constituted a major obstacle to the success of the football team.

The Alouettes were nevertheless brought back to life, thanks to Wetenhall and Smith. On several occasions, Wetenhall and I discussed the futures of our respective teams. Faced with the Alouettes' disastrous results, Wetenhall wanted out. I suggested he move downtown. He might never have dared do it had U2 not booked Olympic Stadium.

Several years later, in 1996, when we were thinking of making our own move downtown, Laurier Carpentier and I envisaged the creation of a megacompany that would merge the Expos and the Canadiens into a single Québécois entity. We also foresaw bringing in a television network and a radio network as partners. It became more and more obvious to us that professional sports teams in Canada, particularly those established in Montreal and part of American-based leagues, were going through a period crucial to their survival. The viability of the Canadiens, just like that of the Expos, was shaky, as much on the ice or the field as on the financial front.

The revenue levels that would allow the teams to hold their own with U.S. teams, even assuming good attendance, weren't there. There was, of course, the exchange-rate problem, with the Canadian dollar fluctuating between 65¢ and 70¢ U.S., and the salaries of players in both leagues, which were ever increasing. Additionally, the contracts negotiated for television and radio rights were probably the least lucrative in North America. The situation in Montreal is unique; most of the French-language television networks in Quebec have tremendous difficulty making a profit. And there is little competition on the radio side, with only one network demonstrating interest in acquiring the broadcast rights. Advertising revenues are extremely limited, with the profit margin close to nil, and the broadcasters have only one policy: take it or leave it. Neither the Canadiens nor the Expos were in a position to impose their own price.

This association would allow us to save substantial money on operations. Common strategies could be established both on the marketing side and on the ticket-sales side. As well, the activities of the two teams would complement each other: the Expos played in the summer, the Canadiens in the winter. If we consolidated both local sports entities into a single unit, we could also attract prestigious corporate support thanks to joint sponsorship and advertising projects.

Under the same umbrella, three companies would have been created. A sports company to manage the Expos and the Canadiens, a real-estate firm to manage the Molson Centre and the new downtown ballpark, and finally an entertainment company.

I discussed the possibility with Jacques Ménard, who told me he had good contacts at Molson. On September 29, 1997, Ménard, Molson advisor Pat Kelly, and I had a meal together, during which I attempted to identify the problems common to the two organizations and the advantages of a merger. At the end of the meal, I suggested we meet again in the near future with Laurier Carpentier and anyone else from upper management who was interested to further explore the merger idea.

I expected Molson to get back to me, but several weeks went by without any news. Then Ménard told me he knew Eric Molson very well and would ask him what he thought of my proposal. Ménard finally came back to me with the news that Molson's priority remained the brewery business and that the company wasn't interested in other issues at that moment.

I was disappointed. I was convinced the Canadiens would have to deal with the same problems that had been assailing the Expos for the past few years, even if they could count on a more solid revenue base and weren't grappling with high payrolls—not yet, at least.

Molson seemed to be unaware of the scope of the problems looming on the horizon. As well, the powerful brewery no doubt considered itself safe from financial risk, wrongly thinking the Molson Centre would generate substantial profits.

I thought the construction of the Molson Centre without a financial contribution from the government was a major error. And the city's administration continued to levy substantial property taxes on the facility, which was owned by hockey club. The lack of collaboration from government authorities had weakened the team's bargaining position.

Perhaps I should have approached more perceptive business-people. In hindsight, when you realize where the Canadiens and the Expos stand, our idea should at least have been of interest. But the Molson executives were convinced we were being too alarmist.

At the time, I believed the future of professional sport in Quebec rested entirely on the formation of a megacompany grouping the Expos, the Canadiens, and—why not?—the Alouettes. I discussed it with Minister of Municipal Affairs Rémy Trudel, who seemed to be interested in exploring it further. The creation of such a company may not have cured all ills, because the problems were enormous. But one thing is certain; the marshalling of our respective forces would have helped us to face the future. And, who knows, we might have succeeded!

Now, in 2002, both the Expos and the Canadiens have been sold to Americans, and their situations in Montreal are worrisome, to say the least. The Expos' shareholders lost everything in an investment that could have brought big returns, while Molson gave up both the Canadiens Hockey Club and the Molson Centre at a bargain price. It is unbelievable that such major changes could have occurred in only three or four years. Under different circumstances, the results could have been much different.

CHAPTER 11

First Meeting with Bernard Landry

Despite the lack of interest in the new stadium from the team's other owners, and their inability to find alternative solutions, I refused to accept the status quo. At any rate, time was of the essence. As I'd explained to Jacques Ménard, putting off the problem would solve nothing; we had to act now.

One of the reasons I'd become involved in this project was to create a legacy. I wanted to leave something tangible behind, a facility baseball fans and sports fans in general could enjoy for years to come.

But I also knew that, for this dream to become reality, I had to have the support of the various levels of government. When we were purchasing the team from Charles Bronfman in 1990 and 1991, the commitment of Quebec premier Robert Bourassa and the support of Montreal mayor Jean Doré had helped to reassure the business community. I intended to go the same route this time.

I requested a meeting with Bernard Landry, Quebec's vice premier and minister of finance. I wanted to brief him on the team's current situation and the expected trends in Major League Baseball over the next few years. Actually, I wanted to repeat to him what I'd already explained to my partners.

On November 28, 1996, Richard Le Lay, my advisor in matters concerning the Quebec government, and I travelled to Landry's offices in Quebec City. But we weren't alone. Ménard had asked me to take Claude Blanchet of the Solidarity Fund to better champion our cause with the minister.

The meeting began well. I outlined the team's situation within the current context in the baseball industry. Landry and his chief of staff, Raymond Bréard, quickly grasped the complex issues involved. Landry, like Bourassa, had been trained as an economist; nothing I told him came as a surprise.

"The way we see it, Mr. Minister, there is only one solution: the construction of a new downtown stadium," I said. "The project is only in its preliminary stages; we have to study the feasibility of the actual project. But we promise to come back and see you as soon as things are clearer. . . ."

Landry appeared to agree with the suggested approach.

That was when Blanchet said, "As for me, I don't believe in this new stadium at all!"

Stunned, Le Lay and I looked at each other. What in the world was he saying? Blanchet was supposed to be there to build us up, not bring us down. Landry and Bréard were also surprised by Blanchet's remark; they were baffled by his outburst. I was furious. Blanchet had just stabbed me right in the back.

Back in Montreal, Le Lay contacted Clément Godbout, whom he knew well, and told him what had happened. Godbout, who ran the Fédération des travailleurs du Québec, from which emanated the Solidarity Fund, was Blanchet's boss. On learning what the man had done, an angry Godbout let fly a string of expletives.

Without the support of the members of the consortium, with the exception of Bill Stinson of Canadian Pacific, but aware Landry was interested in "knowing more" about the downtown stadium project, I decided to go ahead. Landry hadn't said yes, but he hadn't slammed the door on us. As with the purchase of the team, the politicians were being very careful, with good reason.

My concern was mainly with those who should have been my most staunch allies: the members of the limited partnership. Without descending into paranoia, I knew several people had no interest in seeing me succeed in my initiative. I also knew they would let me continue in the hope I would fail, lose face, and be forced to give up my place at the head of the consortium. Several partners wanted me to fall flat on my face in heading up this project. For that reason, following the meeting with Landry, I decided to reduce the stream of information to the partnership to a strict minimum in order to avoid leaks to the media. I found it more prudent to go it alone, with my own management team, obviously.

To ensure the smooth operation of the project, I handpicked a trustworthy group: Executive Vice President of Business Development Laurier Carpentier, Vice President of Operations Claude Delorme, Vice President of Marketing Richard Morency, Vice President of Communications Johanne Héroux, and Vice President of Finance Michel Bussière. To this group was added Richard Le Lay, who continued to advise me on government matters.

The hardest part lay ahead: proving to the government and to my partners, with the numbers to back up our claim, that a downtown stadium was the solution to our endemic problems. We needed solid, verifiable data collected and processed by a reliable accounting firm that boasted an excellent reputation in the business world. I advised my consortium partners that I was making a preliminary amount of $640,000 available to proceed with a feasibility study, and I entrusted Carpentier with the task of supervising the work group.

It wasn't his first challenge. With the Expos since February 1993, Carpentier had worked in the financial field since 1974. A native New Englander, he'd begun his career with the Banque canadienne nationale (now the Banque nationale) in Montreal and in New York, followed by a stint with the Mercantile Bank in both Montreal and Dallas.

I trusted him to lead the group because of his remarkable performance during the new stadium initiative in Jupiter, Florida, a stadium the Expos now shared with the St. Louis Cardinals. It was where the two teams held their training camps each spring.

This project began at the end of 1993, when the Expos were sharing West Palm Beach's Municipal Stadium with the Atlanta Braves. The complex was obsolete, not equipped to handle the requirements of two teams, and required major renovations. And, as the "principal" tenant, the Braves took priority. The Expos had to use secondary fields for their training sessions. And our minor-league training facilities were located at a high school in Lantana, more than 40 km south of West Palm Beach. Other major-league teams were modernizing their facilities, in both Florida and Arizona. We thought the time had come to move into a new stadium.

Rob Rabenecker, in charge of our activities in Florida, Carpentier, and I took on the project. It was a major challenge. We had to convince the government authorities that building a new stadium would serve the interests of the population in that part of Florida. Then we had to find a way to finance construction, find the right building site, draw up the architectural concept, hire a contractor, and deliver it all on time and on budget.

As the downtown stadium project in Montreal was starting up, the stadium in Jupiter was under construction. It had taken more than three years of negotiations with the government authorities and the business community in Palm Beach County before the project became a reality.

At first, the county's political leaders didn't want to hear anything about a new stadium. But Carpentier and I proposed a financing formula that wouldn't cost taxpayers a penny: increasing the hotel tax imposed by the county by one percent. In other words, tourists and visitors would be the ones financing the project. This special tax brought in $26 million of the $27.5 million needed to build the stadium complex.

As part of the agreement, the Palm Beach taxpayers would own the stadium, signing 20-year leases with the two teams that would use it. The Expos and the Cardinals (who replaced the Braves as our cotenants) participated financially by agreeing to reimburse an additional $1.5 million in bonds issued by Palm Beach County at the end of the lease. Operating expenses remained the responsibility of the two teams. We received an additional $1 million by selling the naming rights to the stadium to Roger Dean, a Palm Beach automobile dealer.

Ground was broken on March 6, 1997. Despite the tremendous heat, the various personalities on hand—politicians, businesspeople, media representatives, as well as members of the two ballclubs—all wore suits for the occasion. We were gathered amid pastures and fields of sugar cane, where on occasion I'd seen a few scrawny cows grazing. We were kicking off a project that would benefit all those participating in it. It was, without a doubt, a moment of tremendous pride for the Montreal Expos, and I had a difficult time concealing my pride. We'd just taken a major step and could now consider ourselves a true major-league organization. We'd finally have our own state-of-the-art baseball park, designed, built, and managed by us for the next 20 years.

The deadline was tight, less than a year; the stadium had to be ready for training camp in February 1998. That it was completed within the prescribed time was due in large part to two men: project manager Laurier Carpentier and operations supervisor Claude Delorme.

Everyone came out a winner. Palm Beach County received modern facilities that would benefit its taxpayers. The construction of the stadium gave the city of Jupiter a boost. And the Expos and the Cards benefited from a new stadium that was one of the best.

In addition, the fans of Palm Beach County were charmed. The number of season tickets for our Grapefruit League season rose from 480 to 1,500 with the inauguration of the stadium, and attendance jumped from 52,800 to 90,000. Annual losses of $340,000 suffered at the old stadium were transformed into a $190,000 profit. In other words, a swing of $530,000 U.S.

If a couple of Quebecers had been able to convince the government authorities and business community in Palm Beach County to support the construction of a new stadium, I told myself, there was no doubt the same Quebecers could successfully see a similar project through right at home in Montreal.

Carpentier would put the experience gained in Florida to use in the downtown stadium venture. From the start, I imposed strict guidelines. Every aspect of the studies Carpentier and his team were having prepared would be carefully examined, with the help of the best advisors and consultants available.

115

From ethical and professional points of view, the new stadium initiative had to be beyond reproach. The project team had to be immune to any outside influences to avoid undue pressure. Each member would stick to his or her field of expertise. I'd be the sole spokesperson for the project; I'd be the one who'd brave the storms.

Things were quickly set in motion. While the firm of SNC Lavalin took charge of the engineering studies, the Montreal and Chicago offices of the accounting firm Ernst & Young set out to evaluate the economic returns to be generated by the Expos' presence downtown. A similar mandate was entrusted to the firm of Raymond, Chabot, Martin and Paré. For its part, the Institut national de la recherche scientifique (INRS) analysed the sociocultural impact of a professional sports team. On the architectural side, the project was awarded to Daniel Arbour et associés, which would collaborate with two American firms specializing in baseball stadium design: NBBJ and, later, HOK. Finally, Jean Saine of Saine Marketing would determine the viability of the project in the corporate community. We had to know, for example, if the season-ticket packages would sell, if there would be takers for the corporate suites. Saine Marketing had done the same type of work during the development of the Molson Centre and the du Maurier Stadium project at Jarry Park. While these firms got to work, financial studies were generated to determine exactly the potential revenues of the new stadium, the costs of development and operations, the taxation aspects, and the external financing questions.

Carpentier and his team supervised all of this activity. He and I met often, two or three times a week, to coordinate and refocus, if necessary, the work of the experts. We all continued with our regular duties for the ball club.

In the spring of 1997, the first reports came in. The experts from Ernst & Young declared that economic activity in the order of $170 million per year would be generated by the new ballpark, notably from the 2,100 jobs created and the taxes remitted to the various levels of government. They expected the downtown stadium to bring the governments a total of $73 million in various taxes annually. The experts from Raymond, Chabot, Martin and Paré confirmed the hypothesis set out by their colleagues at Ernst & Young: construction itself would create 3,785 work years and generate $60 million in revenue for the two governments. In terms of economic returns, moving the Expos downtown would bring major benefits.

The impact on tourism was also worth considering. In 1994, a Léger & Léger study we commissioned showed that numerous visitors came to Quebec mainly to attend a baseball game. Many were "day visitors" from Ottawa, Vermont, or upstate New York. But there were also tourists who stayed longer in Montreal and who, consequently, contributed more substantially to the economic life of the area. We could expect that the new stadium would attract an even greater number of these visitors and increase those returns from $40 million to $60 million annually.

The sociocultural advantages also seemed to be obvious. Sylvain Lefebvre and Daniel Latouche of the INRS concluded the presence of a new downtown stadium would entrench Montreal's position among North America's finest cities. As well, we'd free ourselves of the "white elephant" syndrome that tarnished the reputation of Olympic Stadium, long associated with the blunders of the Drapeau-Taillibert era, in much the same way Montreal was trying to rid itself of a similar stain concerning Mirabel Airport. According to the INRS, the presence of a baseball team in a North American city added to the quality of life and represented an attractive corporate element. As well, Montreal is a city that loves to party. The jazz, film, and comedy festivals, Formula One racing, the Tennis Masters Series at du Maurier Stadium—all contributed to this ambience. Downtown baseball was a good fit with the various other summer activities. Lefebvre and Latouche added several other elements that justified the construction of a downtown ballpark, notably the increase in urban tourism or, more specifically, the idea of a city as a "theme park," the importance of "sports tourism" from the United States (where baseball is the favourite sport of 20% of Americans), and so on.

The investigation by the INRS allowed us to expand the scope of a new stadium by positioning it as part of the social and cultural fabric of Montreal. Among other conclusions, Lefebvre and Latouche determined professional sport is an important element of the leisure and entertainment sector; it contributes to the creation and maintenance of a local economy's identity. The economic and sociocultural impacts of a new stadium seemed to be obvious to the researchers, but we needed to measure the effects on the most interested party, the Expos.

At the request of Carpentier and his team, the specialists turned toward the United States, specifically to the baseball industry, to try to predict the economic evolution of this sector over the next 10 years. One thing was certain: players' salaries would continue to rise. They were expected to reach an average of $60 million U.S. per team in 2001 and $72 million by 2007. It was also expected more and more teams would build new facilities. Eighteen new ballparks would be built between 1997 and 2002, engendering a significant increase in both attendance and revenue. From 2003 to 2007, this growth would continue, albeit at a less sustained pace.

Teams that had begun construction on new facilities (about a dozen) had been able to precisely evaluate the revenue generated by their new complexes. With 56% of total revenue tied to the stadium itself (tickets, concessions, and spin-off products), these teams now found themselves among the wealthiest in all of Major League Baseball. Thanks to their new facilities, the owners of these clubs (most of them located in small markets) were able to dig themselves out of the financial crises that had assailed them between 1990 and 1993. And by moving into new, more profitable stadiums, these teams could use the additional revenue generated to increase their payrolls and, consequently, increase their chances of winning more often.

Organizations that didn't take that route would still have to deal with the spiral in salaries without the additional revenues. Those teams would become even poorer and would be unable to compete with the teams that did have new facilities.

Profitable from both the financial and the sociocultural view-points, the move downtown would also allow us to keep up with the current developments in the baseball industry. The "downtown" trend in the United States was our only lifeline. That was all well and good. But where would the new stadium be, and what would it look like?

Daniel Arbour and his associates, along with NBBJ and HOK, were inspired by the new American ballparks even as they took Montreal's particularity into account. In the United States, most of the facilities belong to the public sector, which typically financed about 80% of the construction. The costs of the stadiums ranged between $192 million and $290 million U.S., if they were open air, and between $272 million and $417 million if they were domed or equipped with a retractable roof.

The ballpark proposed by Arbour and his team would cost $250 million Canadian, less than the other projects either already completed or well on their way. But I knew we should really plan for $350 million because of the umbrella roof we wanted to install. I counted on financing the additional $100 million by a special tax on admission tickets.

One morning Arbour and Carpentier invited me to see the model of the proposed stadium. I fell in love with it. Its Renaissance Napoleon III architecture, reminiscent of the old Bonaventure train station, delighted me. Covered with brick, heated seats all located close to the playing field, a 150,000-square-foot terrasse behind right field, a natural-grass surface. . . . Every detail of this stadium, which would hold 35,000 fans, pleased me.

Several potential sites were examined, and, with the help of Arbour and his team, Carpentier and I selected the block bordered by Notre Dame, de la Montagne, St. Jacques, and Peel Streets. From that location, fans would have a magnificent view of the city skyline. Although the plot of land was a bit small, we thought it was suitable. Even more so because it belonged to Canada Lands, a crown corporation. An option on the land was taken out immediately.

It was now Jean Saine's turn to determine the long-term viability of the endeavour. Saine and his colleagues produced three comprehensive surveys, spread out over 1996 and 1997. No fewer than 10,000 interviews were conducted with season-ticket holders, representatives of companies that weren't season-ticket holders, and the public.

The results spoke for themselves. A new stadium could sell 18,545 season tickets, a major increase from the 6,000 at Olympic Stadium at the time. In an "improved" Olympic Stadium, meaning an open-air venue where seating capacity would drop from 45,000 to 30,000, we could sell only 9,908 season tickets. These new commitments would allow us to increase attendance in a significant way. Olympic Stadium was attracting approximately 1.6 million fans per season; the new facility could increase that number to more than 2.7 million.

The downtown ballpark offered several advantages compared with Olympic Stadium: proximity of office towers, boutiques, and restaurants, proximity of all services, no need to travel to the east end of the city, and so on. As well, even if we slightly increased the cost of a ticket, a baseball game would still cost half as much as a hockey game at the Molson Centre.

Saine Marketing concluded by estimating the new stadium could provide us with an additional $50 million in revenue per year. With these new funds, we could finally balance the books and still put a quality team on the field. And, most of all, we'd be in a position to keep our star players.

1987. At training camp in West Palm Beach, Florida:
Claude Brochu with Buck Rodgers, manager of the Expos.

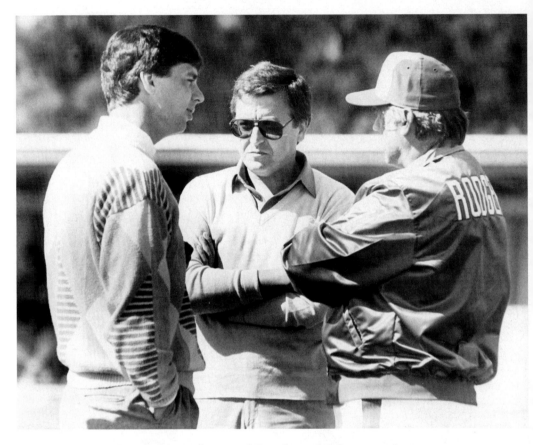

1988. From left to right: David Dombrowski, the general manager, speaking with Claude Brochu and Buck Rodgers.

Early 1990. From left to right: Jacques Ménard and Jean Lajoie of the
Burns Fry team with Claude Brochu, centre.

Michelle, Claude Brochu's spouse, was a regular at Expos games. Here
the couple is seated with Bill White, president of the National League.

1990. Baseball commissioner Fay Vincent during his annual visit
to Montreal; here with Buck Rodgers and Claude Brochu
just before a game.

At a tennis tournament. To Claude Brochu's right are John Beddington of Tennis Canada, world champion Monica Seles, and Roger D. Landry, longtime friend of Claude Brochu.

Claude Brochu and Roger D. Landry with
world-famous tennis player Rod Laver.

November 1990. Press conference at Olympic Stadium,
where the sale of the Expos to the Quebec group was announced.
From left to right: André Vallerand, Minister of Tourism and
minister responsible for the Olympic Installations Board;
Jacques Ménard of Burns Fry; Charles Bronfman; Claude Brochu;
and Jean Doré, mayor of Montreal.

1992. At the Desjardins complex, the unveiling of the new Expos uniform. From left to right, Denis Martinez, Claude Brochu, and Larry Walker.

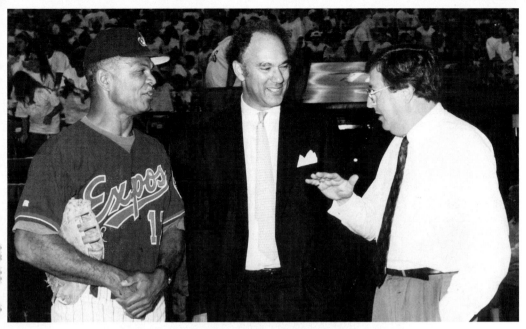

Claude Brochu talks with manager Felipe Alou and Len Coleman,
president of the National League.

A game of golf. From left to right: Mark Routtenberg of Guess Jeans,
Claude Brochu, Mercedes Montreal president Sam Eltes,
and Jacques Demers.

March 1997. Turning the sod at the site of the Jupiter Stadium in
Florida. From left to right: Hall of Fame member Bob Gibson,
St. Louis Cardinals owner Bill Dewitt Jr., Claude Brochu, Cardinals
team president Fred Hanson, and Gary Carter, the great Expos catcher.

February 1988. After Roger Dean's children bought the rights to the name, Jupiter Stadium became Roger Dean Stadium. At the official inauguration, from left to right: Roger Dean, Canada's Governor General Roméo Leblanc, Park Miller, Claude Brochu, Bill Dewitt Jr., and National League president Len Coleman.

Roger Dean Stadium, Jupiter, Florida.

The Expos team that worked relentlessly on the new Montreal stadium project. From left to right: Michel Buissières, vice president, finance; Laurier Carpentier, vice president, development; Claude Brochu; Richard Morency, vice president, marketing; Jim Beattie vice president, general management; Johanne Héroux, vice president, communications, and Claude Delorme, vice president, operations.

Illustration of the Labatt Park project.

Model and illustration of the Labatt Park project.

1995. One of the Expos' great supporters: Tommy Lasorda, former manager of the LA Dodgers and former pitcher for the Montreal Royals, here with Claude and Michelle Brochu.

CHAPTER 12

The Baltimore Example

There was only one issue left to settle to make this dream a reality, but it was a major one: the financing.

We couldn't make the same mistakes that some American teams, notably the San Francisco Giants, had. In structuring the financing for their stadium projects, those teams had allocated a portion of future revenues from advertising and food concessions to the building fund. This isn't a problem at the beginning; the new stadium is always full. But all you need is one down season for a club to find itself in serious trouble. There was no way we'd mortgage the future to finance the new facility. We needed new money. And it could come only from three sources: the business community, the Quebec government, and the federal government, one-third from each. I was also convinced Bernard Landry wouldn't commit to the project without the assurance of participation by the private sector.

For the construction of some new stadiums in the United States, the appeal to the private sector—when it is necessary—comes in the form of the sale of seats or luxury boxes, with the associated right to purchase season tickets. The company puts down a deposit—which is nonrefundable but sellable or transferable—on the purchase of the seat or corporate box while construction is in the planning stages. When the new facility is ready, the company makes the final payment, which gives it the right to purchase the season ticket attached to that seat. If a company decides not to make the season-long commitment, it can't get its deposit back, but it can sell or transfer its right of ownership to another company or individual. The team can also resell the seat or seats freed up by a company that has decided not to acquire the season ticket. This financing formula, commonly known as a "personal seat licence" or "PSL," has proven itself in several American cities.

We elected to use this formula to finance the new facilities. It guaranteed 18,000 season tickets, renewable every season. The advance sale of seats ensured a good level of ongoing participation. A company that invests in a $10,000 seat, for example, will renew its obligation year after year so as not to lose the privilege. The sale of these seats or boxes was an essential condition for implementation of the project, a tangible form of long-term commitment to the team from the corporate community. Without that commitment, it would have been futile to count on the participation of the governments.

Obviously, the approach was key. I rubbed elbows with the business executives in the consortium's circle, and I remembered the difficulties Jacques Ménard and I had when we attempted to interest this group of people in the purchase of the Expos. So we had to go at it carefully and, most of all, avoid scaring away prospective buyers. As well, because we didn't have the necessary resources for a hard-hitting offensive on the business community, we chose to go at it in stages. At any rate, it is never a good strategy to go off in all directions at once. Our approach was logical and well targeted. First we'd secure the commitment of current season-ticket holders, and then we'd approach the team's major sponsors and, finally, the 400 largest companies in Quebec.

Later I'd be criticized for not having approached the public before the business community. That would have been a mistake. The public didn't have the money—at least not enough to play a leading role in the financing campaign. By reeling in the big fish at the start, we were setting up a solid financial base. My first objective was to sell 6,000 seats in the VIP section; they represented half of the dollar amount we required. By setting the example, the business community would influence the public to follow it and bring its own contribution to the project.

I was concerned about the potential participation of the governments, for the stadium couldn't be financed without them. But for the moment, even if their doors were open a crack, I couldn't count on firm commitments. But bringing the subject up at that point would have condemned the project to certain failure. In fact, by letting businesspeople know the governments would also be involved, everyone would adopt a passive attitude. Each side would wait for the other to make the first move.

This discretion about the governments' possible participation didn't mean we were standing still in our attempts to obtain that participation. Quite the opposite. During the weeks devoted to development of the project, we searched for ways to interest the governments in our project without resorting, naturally, to direct aid. We had the same concern during the purchase of the ball club by the consortium in 1991. Suggestions included the imposition of a special visitors' tax, as we'd done in Florida for construction of the Jupiter stadium. This tax would ensure the governments' commitment without upsetting the taxpayers. We also thought of a tourist tax on hotel stays or car rentals. Montrealers probably wouldn't have objected to having outsiders or tourists, many of whom were baseball fans, foot the bill!

We called on Jean-Marc Léger of Groupe Léger & Léger, who'd already produced several surveys for us, to sound out public opinion on this question. The survey would also help us to find paths or solutions, which, even if they weren't necessarily unanimous, would at least reflect majority opinion. I knew the governments were extremely sensitive to public opinion. If we could demonstrate the general population was favourable to a certain type of government aid, it would be that much easier to convince politicians to commit to the project. The results obtained by Léger were very informative. More than half of Montrealers surveyed (51%) believed the governments should get involved financially with the stadium (62% in the case of baseball fans).

I met with Bernard Landry again at the beginning of June 1997—without Claude Blanchet this time! I briefed him on the studies we'd commissioned, the strategy we envisioned, and the results of the surveys conducted by Léger. The minister of finance agreed with the approach we'd adopted. The idea of leaving the Quebec government "in the shadows," at least for now, obviously pleased him. In substance, he told me to focus on the business community; then, based on its contribution, the government would be able to make its contribution. I knew I had an ally in Quebec City when I left that meeting—and not just any ally. Landry was the government's number two man, and Premier Lucien Bouchard trusted him completely, particularly in economic matters.

Reassured about the eventual support of the provincial government—on the condition, of course, that the business community did its part—I turned to the federal government. I received a favourable welcome there as well. The federal representatives were already aware of our financial difficulties. Since 1995, over numerous meetings in Ottawa, I'd made them aware of the trying conditions faced not only by the Expos but also by most of the professional sports teams.

The federal government was directly involved in the stadium project: it owned the land on which we planned to build, managing it through a Crown corporation, Canada Lands. The corporation was prepared to give it to us for the symbolic sum of one dollar. In return, we'd give the various government organizations free advertising in the stadium for 20 years, advertising that had a value to the team of approximately $1 million per year.

Herb Metcalfe of the Capital Hill Group, a consulting firm we'd dealt with for more than a decade, assigned political consultant Jean-François Thibault to our case. Over the next few months, via Thibault, I contacted the advisors to various ministers before meeting with the principal ministers from the Montreal region: Martin Cauchon, Alfonso Gagliano, Marcel Masse, Lucienne Robillard, Pierre Pettigrew, and Minister of Finance Paul Martin. I also met with Jean Pelletier from the prime minister's office.

The final decision was up to Martin, with the assent of Prime Minister Jean Chrétien, of course. But I wanted to ensure the other ministers were also aware of the difficulties involved in managing a professional sports team in Canada. I also wanted to inform them that, in the United States, government help represented up to 80% of construction costs of a new stadium.

As always, the federal government took into account the national context before granting any request for financial support. Whatever it did for the Expos, would it be prepared to do the same for the Blue Jays, eventually, or for any other Canadian professional sports team? One thing was certain: even if Ottawa was open to financial aid, it wouldn't make a move without first confirming the contribution of its provincial counterpart.

I was confident. Thanks to one of my good friends, Jean Carle, the operations chief in the prime minister's office, I knew Chrétien approved of the project and firmly believed in its success. A baseball fan, the prime minister was hardly indifferent to our efforts. Carle and I discussed whether the federal government would participate in the project within the framework of the federal infrastructures program (see appendix, page 237, letter dated April 28, 1998).

Everything was slowly but surely falling into place. The results of the studies and surveys we'd commissioned proved the new stadium would be profitable and solve the team's financial problems once and for all. The federal and provincial governments were receptive to the project, especially since the public favoured a financing formula involving government participation. But everyone agreed on one thing: the success of the project depended on the participation of the business community.

We'd accomplished a lot in six months. Until that point, the work had been done discreetly, far from the spotlight. The time had come to move to another phase: official announcement of the project. A delicate task.

Several partners in the consortium disapproved of the idea of a new stadium. As soon as the news got out, they'd be asked for their opinions. And since they loved to make public statements, we could expect the worst.

To counterbalance these potentially negative elements, we had to make absolutely sure the media understood and endorsed our plan. We therefore invited reporters to take in a Baltimore Orioles game in their new home, Orioles Park at Camden Yards.

We chose Baltimore very carefully. Memorial Stadium, Baltimore's version of Olympic Stadium, hadn't attracted fans for a long time. When the Orioles played in the 1983 World Series, the stands weren't even full. The new stadium, opened in 1992, brought back the fans. As well, in Baltimore as in Montreal, taxpayers had opposed any direct government funding for construction of the new facilities. People in Maryland wanted the government to put money into the schools (people in Quebec wanted the government to support health care). The state therefore created the Maryland Sports Authority, which managed the implementation of a project financed via a special lottery and tax-exempt bonds.

But what impressed the reporters most was attending a ball game in a location that bore no resemblance to depressing Olympic Stadium. At Camden Yards, baseball took on a more human, more accessible dimension. The proximity of the players and the layout of the stands, for example, allowed the public to find once again the ambience lost in large, half-empty stadiums in North American suburbs. "A stadium that smells like baseball," Pierre Durocher wrote in the *Journal de Montréal*. The media representatives were keen when they returned home from Baltimore, even if Durocher doubted I could interest the governments in the project, as the promoters of Camden Yards had managed to do in Baltimore.

At 9:30 a.m. on Friday, June 20, 1997, when I announced our plans, several reporters were already aware of the concept of a new stadium. Having seen the facilities in Baltimore, they had no trouble imagining a life-sized version of the scale model built by Daniel Arbour. The presentation of the model was one of the high points of the press conference. I put my cards on the table from the get-go: "I am not here to convince you at any cost of the necessity of the project," I said. "It is, above all, a business decision. Let us take the time together to examine all the elements and evaluate whether or not they make sense. If they do, let's build the stadium. If they don't, let's forget the whole thing. Leaving an empty stadium for a ballpark that is just as empty will most assuredly not solve anything."

Afterward, I reached out directly to the business community, as Philippe Cantin reported in *La Presse*: "You told us that you would come to ball games if the stadium were located downtown. Now is the time to prove it," he quoted me as saying. Then Cantin quoted New York mayor Rudolph Giuliani, who recognized that the presence of Major League Baseball in his city was profitable from an economic standpoint. "If it's true for New York, it's also true for Montreal," Cantin wrote.

Generally speaking, the media considered I'd delivered my message well. A new downtown stadium, or the Expos were finished in Montreal. "This isn't blackmail but rather simple logic," the Montreal *Gazette* said in an editorial. Reporters also thought I hadn't made the same mistake as former Quebec Nordiques owner Marcel Aubut, who'd demanded help from the government before even finding out whether or not the business community would support him. I posited participation of the private sector as a precondition to the success of the project.

A total success, then. Even if some observers believed my expectations of the corporate community were optimistic, most agreed the project was off to a good start.

Unfortunately, not everyone agreed. When asked about it by reporters the day before the press conference, Premier Lucien Bouchard—even though he hadn't yet been officially approached by the Expos—declared, "When we're closing hospitals, I'm not sure we should be opening stadiums." Bouchard added: "A stadium? We already have a big one, which cost a few dollars and isn't finished being paid for." An emotional comment, a bit of demagoguery, perhaps, put forth without having consulted Bernard Landry, his minister of finance.

I'd just discovered a new opponent.

CHAPTER 13

The Departure of Pedro Martinez

I wasn't discouraged by Premier Lucien Bouchard's reaction, although he could have kept quiet or at least looked into the project before sharing his thoughts with the media. I knew that the dossier was in the hands of Bernard Landry and that the minister of finance continued to support the project. But there was no question of making that support public. In my statements to the media, I asked Bouchard to keep an open mind and not to close the door right away. Simply, I asked him to wait before he expressed his opinion.

At our next meeting, Landry and I, along with our advisors Raymond Bréard and Richard Le Lay, agreed to continue our work discreetly—to move the project forward without stirring up those who opposed it. "Let me lay the groundwork," Bréard repeated. The objective was to prepare the best possible case so the premier could commit to the project without concern about negative reaction from the public.

Speaking of the public, they greeted the project favourably. From May 1997 on, Léger & Léger periodically submitted the results of surveys that confirmed public support for the construction of a new downtown stadium. We made a lot of progress that year. From 44% in August 1997, the project's approval rate climbed to 60% in May 1998. Among francophones, 59% approved of the project in 1998, up from 39% in 1997. Among anglophones, support increased slightly: 60% in 1997, 64% in 1998. The most spectacular progress was registered with men (up from 47% to 70%), especially those between 18 and 24. Their approval rate for the new stadium increased from 35% to 74% in less than a year, a remarkable increase. But it wasn't all that surprising considering young people typically think about the future and older people— those opposed to the project—are more preoccupied by health care and their retirement pensions.

The latest data reassured Landry. Youth, the electoral base of the Parti québécois, agreed with the idea of moving the Expos downtown.

Another result was even more revealing. Among those who approved of the government's participation, 61% approved of the use of part of the income tax paid by the players to help finance the new stadium. That share climbed to 69% among baseball fans. To the minister of finance, these numbers proved the stadium project was "sellable."

I provided Landry with the results of the studies as soon as they were available. The minister's civil servants evaluated and approved the reports and the business plans we presented, even if a few members of the media cast doubt on the numbers put forth in those documents. Landry analysed all the aspects of the project in depth: economic, political, and social. He became more and more convinced the Expos' presence contributed to Montreal's international reputation. For Landry, a baseball team played the same role as a symphony orchestra, for example.

As the dossier progressed normally where the minister of finance was concerned, the team's co-owners, for their part, hardly remained idle. Unfortunately, their efforts were headed in the opposite direction.

Following my decision to study the feasibility of the project, the members of the consortium had remained quiet. Most of them showed little eagerness to support my efforts with the business community and government representatives. From the start, they didn't believe in the life preserver the new downtown stadium represented. They didn't believe I could sell the idea. But they would shortly have to face the facts.

From August 1997, when the financing campaign was launched, to November 1997, more than 1,500 seats were sold for a total of $15.7 million. In less than three months, we'd proved the idea of a new stadium and our method of financing pleased the business community. All we had to show potential buyers were photographs, plans, and a model. We hadn't even begun to build the stadium. There was interest in it; that much was undeniable.

The co-owners remained as resentful as ever in the face of the authority I had over the organization. The question of the new stadium only seemed to aggravate the situation. As Laurier Carpentier and his team continued their work, and Richard Le Lay maintained contact with Quebec City, I heard and witnessed some strange things. I was told certain members of the consortium were conducting meetings that didn't include me—that Pierre Michaud, for example, denigrated the stadium project at every opportunity. Same story from Raymond Bachand, a very good friend of Jacques Ménard's who'd replaced Claude Blanchet as the Solidarity Fund's representative. Same thing from Jocelyn Proteau, Paul Roberge, and Avie Bennett.

What was this smear campaign all about? Beyond the usual issues of power and control, jealousy might have been coming into play. The members of the consortium had seen the respect I'd earned over the past six years with Major League Baseball. Perhaps my contacts, my friendships (not only in the professional sports arena but also in the business, financial, and political worlds in the United States), had sparked their envy in some way. The members of the consortium represented the most prestigious companies in the province, but their expertise and influence were limited to Quebec.

And there was something else. Apparently, I'd become too big for my britches to suit them. They wanted to bring me down, put me in my place, show me who was boss. During a partnership meeting on September 9, 1997, the partners were sceptical about my chances of succeeding, and they wanted to transfer the team outside Montreal for the 1999 season if I didn't succeed.

A discussion then began between my project team and several of the partners on the various methods used to create interest in the project and on the strategy to be used for the promotional campaign. It became clear that, if a sufficient number of seat licences weren't obtained from the corporate base, the project was doomed. It then became critical for several of the partners to determine exactly what the plan would be in that case, given the few remaining solutions and our precarious financial situation.

It was thus decided that at the end of the season the limited partners would hold a special meeting to take stock of the results of the presale campaign. In January 1998, another evaluation would be made of the support obtained and the actions required. A similar evaluation would take place in April. A final decision would be made about the future of the team, and, if we elected to sell, we'd have to proceed in such a way that the transfer of the team be done in time for the 2000 season.

Several weeks later, the partners began to revise their opinions: the downtown stadium project was daring, and perhaps it could succeed, but I wasn't, according to them, the right man for the job. The seat-licence sales were, in their estimation, insufficient. They could do a lot better than I was doing.

From the end of the summer of 1997, the co-owners were on my case. They wouldn't let up until they won. Neither would I.

As the campaign of denigration began, Richard Le Lay and I continued our work with Bernard Landry and his political associates. It was a good thing I could count on my advisor. A regular within the organizations and hallways of power, well versed in the political world, skilful, sensitive to the slightest nuances of vocabulary, Le Lay complemented me well. I was pragmatic, direct, and not very subtle in my approach; I needed the tactician Le Lay at my side if I wanted to be heard by civil servants at the highest levels.

As the weeks went by, I had no doubt Landry and his team wanted the project to become reality. "Let's find solutions," he'd say when we ran up against a problem or difficulty of some kind.

Unfortunately, the premier didn't share this enthusiasm. During a preliminary meeting in Landry's offices on Sherbrooke Street in Montreal, Jean-Roch Boivin, one of Bouchard's closest advisors, listened more or less attentively to my presentation, without asking questions, without showing any interest. Following that meeting, Le Lay and I agreed with Landry and Bréard to keep confidential all of the work being done to secure the government's participation.

Landry was also wary. According to those close to him, he had serious reservations about certain members of the consortium, notably Jocelyn Proteau, Pierre Michaud, and Jacques Ménard. Those businessmen were concerned, he believed, more with their images and their personal interests than with the economic growth of Quebec. In Landry's circle, they were considered as "faux Quebec Inc."

However, as support for the project became reality, the minister of finance increasingly shed his reserve. He promised me he'd communicate with Paul Martin, his federal counterpart, in the hope of forming an alliance. If Ottawa refused, Quebec City was still ready to commit on its own.

To widen my support within the government, Landry suggested I brief some of his colleagues: Serge Ménard, the minister in charge of Montreal, and his successors Robert Perreault and Rémy Trudel, as well as Minister of Tourism David Cliche. Richard Le Lay and I also approached members of the Liberal opposition: Daniel Johnson and Liza Frulla, then party leader Jean Charest, to keep them updated on the project.

Basically, all was progressing as expected. We were too committed to turn back. Our financial situation allowed for no other solution than construction of a new stadium. And time was running out. The Expos finished the 1997 season with disappointing results, on the field as well as in terms of revenue. At 78-84, a winning percentage of .481, we finished fourth in the division and 23 games out of first place. In 1995 and 1996, attendance jumped from 1,309,618 to 1,618,573; only 1,497,609 fans visited Olympic Stadium in 1997. That figure was one of the lowest in Major League Baseball that year.

General Manager Jim Beattie, who'd replaced Kevin Malone, and I met the media in September to update them on the situation. We put our cards on the table; there was no point in trying to hide anything. To Serge Touchette of the *Journal de Montréal*, I said, "We cannot delude ourselves. We're last in the league in everything: last in attendance revenue, last in parking, last in television, etc."

Our financial situation was as dismal as when the players went on strike in 1994. The club lost $11 million in 1997. It lost $7 million in 1996. Barely a year earlier, I'd alerted Ménard and the other members of the consortium about the team's mounting financial difficulties. My predictions were now reality, and we could expect the situation to get worse. One thing was certain: it was becoming more and more difficult to operate in that environment.

I provided Réjean Tremblay of *La Presse* with some troubling data: "Ten years ago," Tremblay wrote, "the Expos had revenues of $33 million U.S. when the Major League Baseball average was $43 million. Ten years later, the Expos' revenues are $37 million U.S., while the major-league average is $73 million."

The perpetual question of salaries was once again raised. With a payroll of barely $22 million, we were a long way behind Seattle ($46 million), Florida and the Los Angeles Dodgers ($52 million), Atlanta ($58 million), Baltimore ($64 million), and the New York Yankees ($77 million).

Our only hope was the new stadium. At the time, 40% of the team's revenues came from the United States, via either the national television contracts or the revenue-sharing system I'd helped to create. "As soon as we have a stadium capable of generating revenues," I explained to Serge Touchette of the *Journal de Montréal*, "we'll be able to reduce the revenue-sharing payments from the United States even as we increase the team's payroll."

Fortunately, I had good news to announce about the financing of the new facility. More than half the corporate boxes (at $110,000 each) had already been sold, which proved that the message sent out to the business community had been heard. And Labatt Breweries had acquired the naming rights to the stadium for the sum of $100 million, payable over 20 years.

Between that point and the opening of the new stadium, it was a matter of trying to survive as a ball club—continuing to rebuild so that, when the new stadium opened, Montrealers would have a winning team. We had to make more trades.

In 1996, Moises Alou and Mel Rojas became eligible for free agency. Since we didn't have the means to offer them the long-term contracts they were understandably asking for, they left the team.

The previous season, Manager Felipe Alou had asked Jim Beattie to trade outfielder Henry Rodriguez, a popular player with the fans. The uncompromising Alou didn't like the player's work ethic and habits. Rodriguez preferred to concentrate on what he already did well instead of making an effort to shore up his weaknesses. Beattie offered him to every team in both leagues. No one was interested.

Then it was Pedro Martinez's turn. Since the controversial trade in 1993, Martinez had developed into a formidable pitcher, just as Dan Duquette had predicted. Everyone had forgotten Delino DeShields, the player whom we'd sent to the Dodgers for Martinez. The 25-year-old athlete distinguished himself in 1997. He was in contention for the Cy Young, an award given to the best pitcher in the National League. He'd ultimately win it. Martinez was without a doubt the best pitcher in Expos history.

During the poststrike fire sale in 1995, I'd told reporters the bleeding would stop with Ken Hill, Marquis Grissom, John Wetteland, and Larry Walker. In the summer of 1997, I told them Martinez wouldn't be traded. When times are tough, you try harder than ever to project a positive image. You have to continue to sell tickets and finish the season despite the hazards. When I stated Martinez would stay until he became eligible for free agency, I sincerely believed that would be the case. But the more the season progressed, the more I doubted it myself.

On September 25, 1997, I called a meeting attended by Jim Beattie, Bill Stoneman, Felipe Alou, and all the coaches. We opened our hearts. We talked about everything: the financial situation, the new stadium project, the makeup of the team, the future of baseball in Montreal. Without my directing the discussions, we arrived at a consensus. We agreed to rebuild the team again—one last time—so we could offer fans a competitive team in 2001 when we moved into our new stadium.

With the exception of coach Jim Tracy (now manager of the Los Angeles Dodgers), everyone agreed to give up Martinez to obtain promising young players. We also suggested trading Mike Lansing, whose back problems might have compromised his career in the short term. It broke our hearts to have to do it. But we all agreed—except for Tracy, who said he was fed up with always having to start over—that there was no alternative if we wanted to present the fans with a championship club in 2001.

Martinez was already eligible for arbitration. He had one year remaining before free agency. It was the right time to trade him. In any case, we would have lost him the following season. The star pitcher couldn't do much for the current squad despite his enormous talent. In two or three years, it would be different, but at that time the team didn't have sufficient depth to support a pitcher of his calibre.

With a heavy heart, I had to renege on the promise made to fans via the media. The reporters seemed to understand the situation in which the team found itself, but the public wouldn't forgive me for going back on my word. During Martinez's last game in Montreal, a fan brandished a poster on which we could read "Trade Claude Brochu!" The frustration of the fans was understandable, but they didn't seem to realize the situation was just as frustrating for us.

By once again sacrificing our best players, I left myself wide open to criticism from a public I absolutely needed to have on my side for the stadium project so that the governments, following the commitment of the business community, would in turn commit themselves. I was in the throes of a painful dilemma. If I caved in to the demands of the fans, I'd put the team in a precarious situation. If I resisted them, I'd risk compromising public support for the stadium project. Either way I'd end up the loser.

Everyone wanted to crucify me because I wanted to trade Martinez, but, surprisingly, fewer than 10,000 fans showed up (out of only 12,309 tickets sold) as the young righthander pitched his heart out on his way to winning the Cy Young Award. Without a doubt, it was a difficult public to figure out.

CHAPTER 14

Opening Arguments

Over that winter, we continued our entreaties to the private sector and the governments. The financing campaign continued to progress, but more slowly, notably because of the infamous ice storm in January 1998. On March 1, I revealed to the media that so far we'd amassed $19.7 million from the private sector (see appendix, chart, page 236). My goal was $100 million, which we hoped to reach by June 30. Mark Routtenberg backed my statements. We needed bigger commitments from the business world, or we'd have to say good-bye to Major League Baseball in Montreal.

Worse still, I felt public support for me was being called into question by the media, at least by some reporters. They no longer had confidence in me because of my "numerous" fire sales. I was no longer able to convince the business world and the governments of the need for a new stadium, they said. Where did that impression come from? It was true the sale of corporate boxes and seats had slowed some, but the progress was still good, and the negotiations with Quebec City and Ottawa were progressing normally.

I realized the attacks against me were multiplying. Mark Routtenberg, who attended the private meetings held by the other members of the consortium, reported to me the tone and nature of declarations made by Jocelyn Proteau, Raymond Bachand, Pierre Michaud, and company. By all accounts, they wanted me off the project. And I was convinced the dissident partners weren't content to limit expression of their reservations about me to closed-door meetings and the media. I was certain their criticisms were being spread in the business world and as far as the premier's office.

Jean Lapierre, the popular morning-show host at CKAC, the top French-language AM station in Montreal, organized supper meetings with Premier Bouchard and representatives of the Montreal business community. Bouchard seemed to appreciate the presence of notable liberals in small groups, behind closed doors, where the issues of the day were debated. Obviously, the Expos and the downtown stadium project were discussed. Pierre Michaud took advantage of the opportunity to denigrate the project, which was "all wrong" and doomed to failure, according to him, as long as I was at the controls. Bernard Landry was informed of this opinion and wasn't very happy that Michaud had spoken against both the project and me to the premier. All the work that had been done was being sabotaged from within. Some of the partners were prepared to do anything to have my head, including destroying the stadium project.

A few months previously, faced with the team's difficult financial situation, most of the members of the consortium had wanted to sell their shares and hand over the club to an American buyer. The idea of a new stadium had seemed completely farfetched to them. Now they wanted the stadium, but they didn't want me to be in charge of building it. What was the reason for this madness? And what was the point of it? How could these basically intelligent people imagine the financing of the stadium would be facilitated by my departure? Obviously, the members of the consortium had convinced each other during their secret meetings that they could do better than I was doing. I might know a lot more than they did about baseball, they told themselves, but there was no way I could teach them anything about the Montreal business world.

Accompanied by Richard Le Lay, I made innumerable presentations to solicit the support of organizations such as the Montreal Chamber of Commerce, Montreal International, and the Greater Montreal Convention and Tourism Bureau. The Chamber of

Commerce asked two of its political-affairs committees, urban development and tourism, to evaluate the project. Both subsequently gave it their support. Both Montreal International president Jacques Girard and Charles Lapointe of the tourism office became valued supporters.

For the next six to eight months, an impressive number of the business world's elite joined a support committee to help me with the project. Joining them were representatives of the industrial parks in the greater Montreal area. As well, 40 to 50 presidents of Montreal companies wrote letters of support in which they encouraged their clients, suppliers, and associates to buy seat licences.

But to the group of dissidents, all of that wasn't enough. At any rate, these appeals weren't made by their "gang" and therefore didn't really count.

The 1998 training camp was wonderful. It featured the inauguration of the new Jupiter stadium. A meeting of the partners was called for February 27, shortly before the official opening, to outline the beauty of the project, the financial advantages, and so on to the partners. I explained the stadium was a first-rate facility, one of the best in Florida. And it wouldn't be a stadium used by the team only in March; it would be a shift in strategy that would blaze the trail for the club for the next 20 years.

For the first time in 30 years, the club would have its major-league and minor-league camps in the same location. And two minor-league clubs would play their regular-season games in the stadium. As well, the scouting and player development offices would be located there, and all the player instructional programs would take place on site. The complex would be used nine months a year, maximizing its efficiency and profitability. The project had raised morale and created a feeling of pride, as much among the players as among management. I believed it was a seminal moment for the club.

The stadium was an integral part of a real-estate development project called Abacoa, located on a 2,200-acre site right off Interstate 95 that included 2,000,000 square feet of space allocated for retail stores, a Florida Atlantic University satellite campus, an 18-hole golf course, and 5,000 homes. The baseball complex was the cornerstone of the entire project; on 110 acres of land, it contained a stadium, two administrative buildings, and six practice fields for each of the two teams.

I emphasized the fact that the complex was the result of a major effort on our part; we'd taken the initiative on the project and guided it to its successful conclusion. The battle had been rough at both the municipal and the county levels. We'd even threatened to back away at one point to achieve the goals we'd set out. Nobody had thought we could succeed. Yet we did.

I then invited Laurier Carpentier, whom I introduced as the project's master builder, to say a few words. After his presentation, I expected an enthusiastic reaction from the partners. But there was dead silence. I was stunned: no applause, no congratulations for Laurier. Nothing. Complete indifference from everyone. Blank faces. It was as though they were merely waiting for me to move on to the next order of business. I suggested it would be appropriate to pay tribute to Laurier. Jacques Ménard then invited all of the partners to officially congratulate him on a job well done. Carpentier tried his best to hide his disappointment, but he was obviously hurt. He had a right to expect the quality of his work would be recognized with a little more enthusiasm. Richard Le Lay and I couldn't understand the partners' behaviour.

It was blindingly obvious the new Florida stadium was of no interest to the partners. At a distance of 3,000 kilometres from Montreal, it left them completely cold. Once more they demonstrated they grasped neither the importance of such a project nor its impact on the organization. As well, they lacked manners, failing to show even the most common courtesy toward those who'd brought the project to a successful end.

Later Le Lay remarked to me that some partners had complained

I didn't give them enough prominence in these types of situations. The private meetings had begun in Montreal, and for those partners who were unhappy and frustrated the success of the enterprise in Florida was of little interest.

What had been accomplished in Florida merited the admiration of all. The leaders of this project had managed to build a thoroughly modern complex 3,000 kilometres from home that received praise from all observers, politicians, and businesspeople in Florida as well as members of the professional baseball community. The public and the media in the United States had recognized their professionalism and expertise. But back in Montreal, this undeniable success was greeted with dead silence. We can be so provincial at times.

The Carpentiers and Delormes of the world, under my direction, didn't—in the eyes of some—have the necessary talent to head the new downtown stadium project in Montreal. We had to find other means of support to get there. Jacques Ménard (who now believed in the new stadium project!) called on Jean Coutu, whose chain of pharmacies was ubiquitous in Quebec. An accomplished entrepreneur with an excellent reputation with the public, Coutu was the ideal man to inspire confidence in the business world. For my part, I approached Serge Savard, whose reputation as a professional hockey player and experienced businessman was known to all. On March 10, 1998, Coutu, Savard, and Lynton "Red" Wilson, chairman of the board and CEO of BCE, agreed to become copresidents of the support committee.

I'd been the sole spokesperson for the project to that point. Others had issued statements, and my team was taking on an enormous amount of work, but I was always the one who defended the new stadium, alone, in front of the media. Participating in the press conference from Florida, where I was attending training camp at the Jupiter complex along with Coutu, I said I was happy to see the business world mobilize behind the project. For his part,

Jocelyn Proteau, who admitted having been against the stadium project at the start, confirmed he was now "convinced of its necessity." Jacques Ménard confirmed we expected to raise $85 million from the private sector.

Already the media were describing the members of the support committee as the "saviours" of the project, which apparently was shaky because of my "bad reputation." Réjean Tremblay of *La Presse* even wrote about a "major event in the sporting and . . . economic life of Montreal." Even though I was hurt by these attacks and insinuations, I had no intention of responding to them. What mattered to me was the success of the financing campaign. Nothing else.

I didn't really expect Coutu, Savard, and Wilson to lead the sales effort. My team would do that work in the field. Their roles were to be spokesmen, boosters, to reassure the public. We also wanted to show the business community we were supported by leaders from within its own ranks.

As it turned out, Coutu's talents as a salesman didn't exactly come to the fore. Back in Montreal after his winter holidays, he suggested organizing a cocktail party to which he'd invite representatives of the pharmaceutical companies. We were thrilled. Coutu was the largest purchaser of pharmaceutical products in Quebec; certainly, he'd have some pull with that clientele. But everyone quickly became disenchanted. Organization of the event was slapdash from beginning to end; the invitations were sent out late, for example. The result was that few people confirmed their attendance at the cocktail party, which Coutu ultimately had to cancel.

The biggest pharmacist in Montreal seemed incapable of organizing a simple cocktail party. And this was the man to whom we'd just entrusted the copresidency of the support committee. The "saviour" obviously couldn't save much.

Our sales staff ended up making 94% of the sales of seats and corporate boxes. Coutu and the co-owners sold five percent, mostly to themselves. Mr. Coutu seemed all talk, no action. His signing on with the project was the first time he'd shown any interest in baseball. He knew nothing about it, but he had no qualms about offering his opinions and teaching everyone a lesson.

One day, at the stadium in Jupiter, Coutu took a shot at Roger D. Landry, the publisher of *La Presse*, who was attending a game with my wife, Michelle, and me. "*La Presse* doesn't do enough to help the Expos," he said to Landry.

Landry wasted no time responding. "Hey, do I tell you how to sell your little pills?"

Michelle and I were surprised by the publisher's direct response. She told him he might have been a bit harsh.

Landry answered, "You'll see. . . ."

It was obvious to all the next six months would be decisive for the future of the stadium project and, by extension, the Expos in Montreal. I'd given myself until June 30 to raise the necessary funds from the business community, but the real deadline was the end of September. By then, the seat-licence sales had to reach a high-enough level to give the project credibility. By then, we had to reach agreements with the provincial and federal governments. In other words, it was now or never.

Despite the urgency of the situation, and despite my silence, the co-owners continued to attack me in their by-now semisecret meetings, with the media always waiting outside the door. Proteau, Bachand, Michaud, and now Ménard complained incessantly, criticized my slightest initiative, and talked endlessly about subjects far beyond their understanding. They were sitting around the table blowing smoke up each other's asses, I thought with a laugh. During these sessions, they threw out ideas, invented solutions, put together plans, and imagined plots against them, and none of it made any sense.

Things went even further. An article published in the *Journal de Montréal*, citing "an anonymous source close to the situation," declared it would be improper for the government to advance

$150 million for the construction of a stadium without a change in the structure of the current limited partnership, which gave full powers to the general partner.

Another voice joined the chorus, that of Coutu. As copresident of the support committee, he participated in this fight without even owning a share of the team, having declined to become involved back in 1991. Not that you could have guessed that by the way he was acting.

The other co-owners seemed to be pleased to have this rabble-rouser in their midst. While Proteau, Bachand, and Michaud, to name three, were only delegates from the companies or organizations they represented and constantly had to worry about the images they projected, Coutu answered to no one but himself. A self-made man, he had total control of his company. He could say anything he wanted without worrying about being chastised by his Board of Directors. And he wasn't the least bit shy about doing just that.

All the frustration accumulated over the years seemed to be diverted toward the stadium project. The other owners accused me of hurting the financing effort with my attitude. They attacked me on all fronts.

On the TVA network's *Salut Bonjour* television show, journalist Claude Picher reported a stunning piece of news to the viewers. According to "confidential" information, new financial backers were ready to invest in the Expos to bail out the team. It was a rumour, we learned later, thrown out into the public domain by Coutu himself. For what purpose? I didn't know. At any rate, no new investor came forward. I began to figure out from all this that Coutu was merely the spokesman for the group. It had been his idea, but it had also been the dissidents' idea. During their private meetings, they'd discussed expanding the group of investors to eliminate me and finance the stadium project. Coutu had simply let it slip in front of the journalists.

This false information caused major harm to the financing campaign. Believing "saviours" to be on the horizon, several companies ready to come aboard decided to wait. A normal reaction under the circumstances.

Nonetheless, the sale of seat licences continued to progress. We were now at $27.1 million, up from $19.7 million in March. It was a remarkable result obtained primarily by our sales staff. While the partners were pumping each other up in their campaign against me, they neglected to put any effort into the new ballpark project.

The attacks against me, notably from Coutu, intensified over the summer. During meetings, he constantly challenged the strategy my team and I had mapped out. He never stopped saying "Give me numbers, give me numbers," as I recall. I gave him numbers: numbers on the project's financing, numbers on the progress of sales. Either he didn't understand the numbers, or he didn't like them. He would then go back on the attack.

Even though we were talking about a crucial step toward obtaining credit from the banking institutions, Coutu opposed the seat-licence program and the contract that bound the buyers. His objection was that they received nothing for their money other than the right to buy season tickets. He found the contract too restrictive. But we couldn't do it otherwise. If the contracts weren't binding, the banks would never agree to lend us the money for construction of the stadium based on those contracts.

"Who will own the stadium?" Coutu would ask that question incessantly during these meetings. He apparently refused to understand that the question of ownership of the stadium was not pertinent at that stage of the financing. It was premature. For the moment, Laurier Carpentier and I were searching for an ownership formula that would exempt us from municipal taxes and sales taxes on construction costs. The question of ownership of the stadium itself would be resolved at a later date.

Coutu didn't want to hear any of it. In his mind, this question was critical. He demanded guarantees I was unable to provide. He even threatened to publicly denounce me if he didn't get answers to his questions. It was a threat Coutu would shortly make good on.

The previous year's trip to Baltimore with members of the

media had been a success. I decided to repeat the experience with 70 representatives from the business and political communities to make them aware of the advantages of Camden Yards. Montreal International, an organization whose mandate is to promote Montreal abroad, collaborated in the initiative.

But just prior to our departure, Coutu was the guest of radio morning man Paul Arcand on CKAC. On his own, without any prompting from Arcand, Coutu began to talk against me. "He is no longer the man for the job," claimed the pharmacist who also claimed in his advertisements that you'd find it all at his stores, "even a friend." His inflammatory remarks had just cost him one friend. "He has to go, he has to step aside," Coutu added. The closed-door war the pharmacist had been waging against me had now moved to the public domain, to the detriment of all who were diligently working on the stadium project.

The next morning, as I prepared to join several representatives of the business community at our project offices at Windsor Station, I noticed my photograph on the front pages of newspapers, with Coutu's accusations taken up by reporters. I was furious. His aggressive and vindictive attitude was completely inappropriate. I was prepared to take all the critical slings and arrows the partners threw at me, but I'd tried to minimize the media's involvement in the debate. Now Coutu had done exactly the opposite.

I'd had enough of the moaning and the tirades from the good pharmacist. This time he'd gone too far. I wished only one thing, that he'd fade into the woodwork once and for all so the sale of boxes and seats could begin again.

My first reaction was to respond to his attacks, but my advisors told me not to fall into his trap. If the matter degenerated into a personality conflict, the financing campaign would surely be affected. But I had to react in some way.

At Windsor Station, I approached the microphone. In front of me were representatives of the business and political milieus who were all aware, obviously, of Coutu's statements. I had to convince them to trust me. "His statements are unacceptable," I said in a firm voice. "You cannot agree with a project and then criticize it. . . . I am not the important one here. It is the stadium issue that matters. Remember what I am about to say to you: I intend to work on this project until the end and to succeed." In closing, I sent a message to Coutu. I believed he must resign from the support committee. "I cannot work in a situation where the actions of some could hurt the project," I said. Coutu was helping to make a mess of the new downtown stadium project.

The trip to Baltimore had been a success, but back in Montreal I once again found myself in the eye of the hurricane. The newspapers were reporting Coutu was the spokesman for Proteau, Michaud, and Roberge. He was saying aloud, publicly, what the owners were whispering among themselves.

As Jacques Ménard watched the quarrel explode in the public domain, he carefully aligned himself behind Coutu. Ménard accused me of being too tough on him. All the while giving the impression he supported me, he declared to Marie Tison of La Presse canadienne that it "was necessary to keep all the important people who were in favour of the construction of a downtown stadium on board." Later, to Bertrand Raymond of the *Journal de Montréal*, Ménard said the best way to help me would be to "remove" from me "the unbearable burden that is the complete responsibility for a community project."

I had no intention of resigning. I was the one who'd kept the project afloat since the beginning, the one who'd attempted to convince the partners of its feasibility. I was also the one negotiating with Quebec City and Ottawa, the one who continued to work with Bernard Landry to get the provincial government on board.

The underhanded attacks launched by Coutu, with the support of several members of the consortium, were proof my opponents cared more about my departure than construction of the new venue. It was as though they were using this project to settle accounts with me. That the attacks were also aimed at my management team made me even more furious. Laurier Carpentier, Richard Morency, and the others were working flat out to keep the momentum going forward despite the indifference of the consortium members.

At that point, Ménard and friends believed that the downtown stadium was essential and that only they could build it and, as a consequence, run the Expos. Fortunately, my position was unassailable. The partnership agreement, the one everyone had signed, was clear: I held all the authority. And I couldn't be ousted without the approval of Major League Baseball. Regardless of the methods used, the partners couldn't get rid of me unless I agreed to resign. And I had no intention of doing that. My firm stance on the matter irritated them even more, and they intensified their attacks. They increased the pressure on me in the hopes of seeing me crumble and give up the fight. And, of course, they brought the media into that quest.

Over the summer, the various partners began feeding "exclusive information" to certain reporters, always under the cover of anonymity. These "reliable sources" claimed to have the real story about the hot issue of the Expos' future.

In the Montreal *Gazette*, columnist Jack Todd wrote, ". . . the Expos ownership group has had more leaks than Ken Starr's Whitewater investigation. Led by human sieves Jacques Ménard and Mark Routtenberg (the most public Deep Throats since Linda Lovelace), so many things have been said that the public has the impression that this particular charge is being led by General Confusion."

Most of the reporters, in both languages, participated in the escalation. I had too much power, my communications plan was dreadful, the sale of seat licences wasn't progressing well, the business community was slow to fall into step, and the squabbles within the partnership were intensifying, proclaimed the newspapers.

The madness didn't stop there. Apparently, I'd also told the people of Quebec to "piss off" by concentrating my efforts on the business community; my image was tarnished by the loss of Pedro Martinez and Henry Rodriguez. The public wanted me out. I had to leave. I was poorly served by my staff. I was guilty. I was unpopular with the media. I could do nothing right. I was incompetent. I was stupid.

Who were we talking about here? A war criminal? A serial killer? Hardly. I was merely someone who believed in his ideas and defended them. But the media didn't burden themselves with the subtleties. The Expos had to get rid of me, they concluded. Besides, Ménard had all the attributes required to take over. The newspapers went even further, ascribing to me all the evil intentions in the world. As Serge Touchette of the *Journal de Montréal* explained, ". . . his image, his credibility, his way of seeing things, his way of doing things. . . . The locomotive en route towards downtown already has travelled a considerable distance, and suddenly new conductors wanted to take the wheel."

The members of the consortium were so successful in denigrating me with the media, and consequently with the public, that I feared for my safety. All you need is one hothead. . . . I therefore decided to hire a bodyguard, former police officer Robert Laird, who'd also serve as a driver until the situation calmed down.

The members of the consortium had by now started to enjoy this smear campaign. And they weren't shy to pile it on. They openly attacked the seat-licence plan with the business community. According to the co-owners, a more broadly based financing plan would have been more useful and might have more easily convinced the government to inject funds. This was great in theory. But the partners had nothing concrete to propose. How do you reach the public? What initiatives should be adopted? It's easy to criticize, but when criticism doesn't result in solutions it hurts the project as a whole.

The most stunning thing about this verbal escalation, about this campaign of destruction, was the complicity of the media. Proper journalism requires a lot of research, investigation, verification of sources of information. Normally, reporters don't take the statements of someone as truth without first trying to get to the bottom of the matter to understand that person's motivation for making the statements. It is, after all, supposed to be a search for the truth. But at least where I was concerned, the media gave unlimited credibility to all the leaks, all the moles, all the "deep throats" who came forward without first checking the statements. Reporters desperate for fresh news welcomed with open arms any "reliable source"—even an anonymous one—who had something to say.

I responded to none of those attacks. On the one hand, secure in my position as head of the Expos, I didn't have to worry about job security. On the other hand, Bernard Landry and I had agreed not to make our negotiations—which were progressing well—public. In returning fire, I risked compromising my work with the minister of finance. Anything I said on the subject would spark negative reaction in the media the following day. I couldn't win at that game.

But I also had no intention of stepping aside. That idea never crossed my mind. Thanks to my knowledge and expertise, thanks to my support team, I knew I was the only one who could bring the project to term. I was the only one sufficiently motivated to get it done. My partners were working at it like dilettantes, concerned more with their own interests than with the fate of the ball club.

There was also no question of changing the structure of the limited partnership. Major League Baseball would never accept my putting any measure of control in the hands of the consortium. At any rate, after what had just happened, I'd lost all confidence in my partners.

I therefore chose to keep quiet, especially since Bernard Landry continued to assure me of his support. I also had another ally, Roger D. Landry. Since the beginning of this whole affair, the publisher of *La Presse* had refused to cave in to the madness that had overtaken the team's co-owners. And, it must be said, Landry and I had known each other a long time. He worked in the Expos' marketing department when John McHale was president. I was at Seagrams then. We became friends then, and we were still close as I came under siege.

Landry would regularly call my office and offer his support. "Let it roll off your back," he advised me. "Let them get worked up. You're the one who controls the situation. They can't do anything to you, and they know it. . . ."

Those calls encouraged me; I felt very much alone that summer. I appreciated Landry's gesture, especially because he had relationships with several of the co-owners, including Pierre Michaud, who'd never hidden his opposition to me. Landry and Michaud were both members of the Club des Quinze (the Group of 15), which gathered some of Quebec's elite once a month to talk openly about various subjects. Everything said in those get-togethers was "off the record." I'd even been invited to one of their gatherings to present my ballpark project.

Landry was loyal to me. And he'd never been able to stand Jacques Ménard, whom he thought to be a big talker, nothing more. But despite his loyalty, he didn't believe in the stadium project! He looked at the question in a more global context. Taking into account the weakness of the Canadian dollar and the lower standard of living in Montreal, he believed we couldn't afford to keep a professional baseball team. I understood his point of view, but I still believed we could pull it off with tight management.

In addition to the two Landrys, I had other allies. The first was Serge Savard. The night before the trip to Baltimore, when Jean Coutu vented to the newspapers, Savard came to my defence. "He planned and structured the stadium project from the start," Savard told Bertrand Raymond of the *Journal de Montréal*. "We have to trust him. He hasn't done a bad job up to now. It would be best to get behind him."

For his part, Clément Godbout, president of the FTQ and the Solidarity Fund, wasn't worried about supporting me even if Raymond Bachand, his representative, was one of those in the consortium who opposed me. Godbout was hard on Coutu. To Yvon Laprade of the *Journal de Montréal*, talking about Coutu, he said, "He is sabotaging Brochu at a very bad time. We have a collective responsibility to avoid drama. Instead of gumming up the works, the business community must get involved and invest." He was right. Instead of collaborating with me, my partners preferred to engage in trench warfare—with disastrous results.

Ménard was taking up more and more space in the media during this period. To reporters, he projected the image of a mediator between the dissident partners and club management. In the journalists' opinion, Ménard appeared to have "solutions" to the alleged slowdown of the seat-licence campaign. "The project would be better served by being better presented to the public and the small- and medium-sized companies," he said. "Some people have approached me to tell me they would join me in a restructured project and would put their money in." A specialist of the cliché and the pithy reply, Ménard became the favourite of several reporters who fell for his statements without even questioning them. Slowly, he established himself as the "saviour" of the stadium project, the one who was "sacrificing himself" to get the project back on track. As for me, I was acting only to line my pockets.

Ménard wanted Savard to be identified as the headliner for the financing campaign. I understood Savard was popular with the public, and I'd have agreed to give him more responsibility. But it had to be understood I'd remain the ballpark's master builder, as well as the boss of the Expos, as dictated by the partnership agreement and the executives of Major League Baseball.

To Jean-Philippe Décarie of the *Journal de Montréal*, Ménard at one point declared the members of the consortium had decided to "tone down the differences they might have about Claude Brochu." He even added Coutu had provisionally withdrawn from the support committee and would return when he received the answers to his questions. Ménard's statements suggested harmony had returned to the partnership. The truth was quite different.

CHAPTER 15

A Meeting at the Bunker

At the end of August 1998, Vice President of Marketing Richard Morency revealed to Philippe Cantin of *La Presse* that the club's seat-licence sales had reached $40 million, nearly halfway to the initial objective of $80 million to $100 million. This amount was remarkable since construction hadn't yet begun. "The experiences in other stadiums have shown us that sales increase even more once the project starts," Morency said. "In two days, we have sold $500,000 in seat licences."

Until then, the public hadn't been targeted by the financing campaign. We wanted first to interest the governments, then solicit the support of the business community, and finally approach the baseball fans. That time had come. Through a media advertising campaign, we invited the team's fans to invest $299 each in the stadium project. Every person who paid that amount would have his or her name engraved on one of the bricks in the new stadium.

The public finally approached via an original campaign, the business community reassured and interested once again in the stadium project, we were now ready to reap the benefits of our efforts with the governments. I was confident.

All through the month of August, with attacks coming from all sides, Bernard Landry never wavered from his promise to finance, in some fashion, the new stadium. The minister of finance didn't allow himself to be intimidated or turned off by the attacks from Coutu and company. During this period, we continued our dialogue with Landry. On August 31, he told CKAC's Paul Arcand we were proceeding toward a solution for financing the new stadium. "A solution that will not upset anyone," Landry said.

The next day, my advisor, Richard Le Lay, received a call from Hubert Thibault, Premier Lucien Bouchard's chief of staff. He asked Le Lay why we hadn't asked to meet with the premier about the new stadium. Le Lay was surprised. He didn't understand the reason for Thibault's call. Le Lay explained to Thibault he'd kept André Bellerose, another one of Bouchard's advisors, informed of the progress of the project. Bellerose had told Le Lay to wait, that he'd let him know when the time was right to go and see the premier. Landry's group had also kept Bouchard informed of our discussions. Surely, Thibault knew that. But he suggested Le Lay send a letter to Bouchard as soon as possible requesting a meeting. He even proposed inviting Coutu, which surprised Le Lay even more. What was going on? Something wasn't right.

I prepared the letter. The following day, September 2, Jacques Ménard, Serge Savard, Richard Le Lay, and I headed to Lucien Bouchard's offices, referred to as the "bunker," on Grande Allée in Quebec City. I'd have liked to invite FTQ president Clément Godbout, but he was in Europe. Godbout had warned me it was entirely possible Bouchard would say no, but he'd leave us an opening. The premier is a lawyer by profession, a negotiator. From there, we'd work on widening that opening.

The four of us were ushered into a windowless conference room. We waited several minutes before the door opened and Bouchard entered, followed by Jean-Roch Boivin, Hubert Thibault, and a few other employees. Last to arrive were Bernard Landry and his chief of staff, Andrée Corriveau.

I was pleased to see the minister of finance, but I immediately realized something wasn't right. Landry seemed to be avoiding my glance. He was nervous, agitated, and red faced—as though he were furious about something.

We'd later learn that barely an hour before our meeting Bouchard had called Landry and Corriveau to his office and taken the dossier away from his minister of finance. An incredible, unheard-of move. The premier would take charge of the project from that point on, which explained Landry's attitude during that meeting. In a power play only Bouchard knew the reasons for, he'd treated his principal lieutenant in extraordinarily cavalier fashion.

We suspected nothing.

"We're listening," Bouchard said to us.

I described the project and emphasized its importance for Montreal. Of course, the question of financing and the participation of the government were at the centre of the presentation.

From time to time, I looked over to Landry. He sat there, arms crossed, staring straight ahead. He still seemed to be angry. He wouldn't utter a single word during the meeting.

At one point, Ménard, no longer able to contain himself, intervened. He went on a lengthy diatribe, as was his custom. In this type of situation, Ménard seems to be incapable of synthesizing his thoughts. He talks, talks, talks, as if he enjoys listening to the sound of his own voice. Usually, it doesn't matter. But here, in front of the premier, the danger was that we might run out of time before we completed our presentation. Suddenly, Ménard said, "Obviously, we cannot be sure that the Expos will survive in Montreal, even with a new downtown stadium. . . ."

A major blunder. Richard Le Lay, seated next to Ménard, gave him a well-deserved kick under the table to shut him up. But it was too late.

Bouchard refused to commit his government to the new stadium project. "We have to make societal choices," he said. "We may not even be able to afford the Canadiens."

It was an unenlightened decision. The premier's office had only superficial knowledge of the issue and was preventing Landry, who did have the required competence, from acting with full knowledge of the facts. What enraged me most was that Bouchard had completely disregarded the work done by Landry and his team. He said no without even knowing why.

We'd been set up; we'd fallen into a trap sprung by the premier on his minister of finance. Today, I admit, we made the mistake of rushing to the meeting convened by Bouchard. Had we refused to meet with him, or postponed the meeting, Landry and his group might have had the time to finalize negotiations with our team, and the government's participation would have been confirmed. But Bouchard wanted nothing to do with the stadium project. His advisors recommended he turn us down, especially Jean-Roch Boivin, the one responsible for the Expos dossier with the premier's office. Boivin also closely monitored Hydro-Québec, whose chairman of the board was Jacques Ménard. Members of the partnership had also advised Bouchard not to commit to the project as presented. The premier wanted to act quickly because he wouldn't be able to reverse directions. But what pretext could he have possibly invoked to remove Landry from the dossier? Perhaps an urgent meeting requested by the Expos' representatives.

If, for the public, the Expos' misfortunes were summed up by two crucial moments in the history of the club—its elimination on Blue Monday in 1981 and the players' strike in August 1994— I thought we had to add a third date: September 2, 1998. That night, in the conference room at the bunker, the stadium project died. The team was on life support. It was the beginning of the end.

At the Michelangelo restaurant in the Quebec City suburb of Sainte-Foy, where the four of us found ourselves after the meeting, the atmosphere was funereal. Serge Savard forced himself to encourage everyone. "We must keep on fighting," he said. "This doesn't mean it's over. . . ." I nodded. I pretended to believe it, but I knew it was hopeless. I ate, but with little appetite, going back over the meeting in my head, trying to understand what had just occurred.

No doubt the disputes had eroded the still-tentative confidence of the people in the new stadium. Everyone waited with bated breath, content to watch this embarrassing soap opera unfold. What a mess. The leaders of the province's business world were ripping each other apart in public and in the halls of government.

Clearly, some of the partners had denigrated the project to Bouchard and his team. They'd made sure the provincial government would never support the project. How could they undertake such a smear campaign without considering the reputation of the ball club itself would be caught in the crossfire? How could they believe for a moment they could start over after destroying all the positive elements of the project, alienating the Expos' staff, ridiculing the marketing efforts, and losing the confidence of both the public and the business community? Beyond the contemptuous arrogance of the dissident members of the consortium, their efforts were simply thoughtless and foolhardy. There was no explanation to justify the suicidal practices of some of the partners.

A few days after the meeting with Premier Bouchard, I had lunch with Clément Godbout and Henri Massé of the FTQ at the Mount Royal Club in Montreal. I was down, but I couldn't help but see the humour in the presence of two noted unionists in that bastion of hard-line capitalism. "Call a strike!" Godbout said. That was the union leader in him talking. When negotiations are going nowhere, you have to go to the next step: the threat of a strike.

For us, that threat translated into putting the team up for sale. The important thing was to put pressure on the opposing party. By announcing the immediate sale of the team—something we had no intention of doing, at any rate—we'd push the government to go back on its negative decision.

"I agree with Clément," Massé said. "Especially with the elections coming up. . . ."

I took a deep breath. The two men were right, but I knew the co-owners would never agree to "put pressure" on the government to try to get things moving. Even if the co-owners did agree, the premier's office would immediately be informed of our strategy. As well, I believed several dissident members of the partnership already had an agreement with Bouchard not to make the Expos an electoral issue.

Lucien Bouchard's decision was a lethal blow to our efforts. Even if the media judged the project had been poorly sold, we still found the premier's reaction difficult to accept. Bernard Landry and his team, in concert with the Expos' management, had come up with a financing formula in which the stadium would be partially paid for by the players' income taxes. This way the taxpayer would pay nothing. Three weeks before the September 30 deadline, Bouchard's refusal was a shot below the belt. And, in the wake of the decision in Quebec City, Prime Minister Chrétien's federal government also closed its doors to us, on September 9, barely a week after the meeting at the bunker.

Three distinct phases marked the evolution of the dossier at the federal level. There was a receptive attitude when I first presented the project. Then, as soon as I began to be attacked and the dissension within the partnership became public, the federal government started to dither, began to have misgivings. The third phase was the "no" from Quebec City, which incited Ottawa to say "no" as well.

I was certain we couldn't recover from Bouchard's decision, but I refused to give up immediately, especially because the premier's decision didn't meet with unanimous approval.

Personalities such as former Parti Québécois minister Claude Charron and Denis Coderre, an MP for the Chrétien government and a member of the committee on sport, had already expressed their support in the media for the Expos and the stadium project. Later, however, Coderre would endorse the negative response from Prime Minister Chrétien.

After Jean Doré, Jacques Duchesneau, also a candidate in the upcoming Montreal mayoralty elections, confirmed his intention to help with construction of the stadium through the Programme de coopération industrielle de Montréal, a municipal initiative. Mayor Pierre Bourque was also in favour of the project. And Bourque asked that the September 30 deadline be pushed back to allow more time for prospective investors to come forward.

For his part, Quebec opposition leader Jean Charest exhorted Bouchard to revise his position. And Clément Godbout of the FTQ pleaded with the business community to "wake up" before it was too late.

Baseball authorities also came forward. National League president Leonard Coleman arrived in Montreal to come to my aid.

The fans held a support protest. Close to 1,000 people gathered at the site of the future stadium, posters in hand. The Expos' employees also demonstrated but in front of the Hydro-Québec building where Bouchard's Montreal offices were located.

The most hard-hitting encouragement came from economist Pierre Fortin and urban planner Sylvain Lefebvre, who stated that a "financial contribution from the State was perfectly justifiable." Fortin's helping hand came too late, but his impeccable reputation gave the statements a lot of credibility.

During this period, unfortunately, the consortium's dissidents continued their attacks on me. Once again, it wasn't a concerted effort, a planned offensive. Each partner did his own thing; it was pure anarchy at the heart of the partnership.

Jean Coutu, who'd withdrawn following his dispute with me, reappeared. He repeated the mantra about my "excessive powers." He said he'd be willing to invest in the project "but not in the current situation." In other words, he told the members of the consortium, "Get rid of Claude Brochu, and you'll get my money."

Mark Routtenberg went even further. He showed the *Journal de Montréal* the club's financial statements, which indicated a loss of $4 million in 1998 and a total of $37 million in losses since 1991. The purpose of such an initiative left me perplexed.

Strange. Little by little, the contagion struck everyone in the group. After Ménard, it was Routtenberg who began to attack me. I'd been even closer to him than I'd been to Ménard. Routtenberg was a close friend, an ally within the consortium, the only one who truly loved baseball. He was the only one of the group my wife, Michelle, and I saw socially, after work, along with his wife, Frema. He said he'd vouch for my integrity with the other members of the consortium. I wasn't the Machiavellian character people were portraying. My only problem, according to him, was my . . . incompetence. I hadn't done things properly. The moment he said that, our friendship died.

CHAPTER 16

Good-Bye, Felipe?

The Expos' manager was already in his seventh season when the news broke. "Felipe Alou—Leaving," or some similar headline, hit the newspapers in September 1998.

Alou had captured the hearts of Montrealers since replacing Tom Runnells in 1992. On the field, the 63-year-old Dominican had performed impressively. In August, he'd overtaken Buck Rodgers as the winningest manager in team history. Over the course of those years, Alou had remained faithful to the team that had given him his opportunity. But he hadn't always accepted our management philosophy. Every time we made a trade that cost him a veteran, Alou would call our approach into question.

He was quite a personality. All you needed to do to understand him was listen to what he said to reporters during his daily sessions with them. Those informal press conferences allowed him to spout "off-the-record" opinions on virtually every subject. In principle, the media weren't supposed to report those comments, but they'd eventually find their way into print. Alou wasn't reluctant to more or less openly criticize the team's management; he particularly reproached Jim Beattie for not consulting him on player transactions.

Named general manager in October 1995, Beattie had been the Seattle Mariners' director of player development since 1989. But he'd also played in the big leagues for nine seasons as a pitcher for the Yankees and the Mariners. Beattie knew his stuff. Unfortunately, his relationship with the media wasn't nearly as solid as Alou's.

163

The journalists never questioned the manager's statements. They were scared of Alou. They were afraid they'd be "punished" if they contradicted him. He could have refused to talk to them, to grant them interviews. Over the years, Alou became a master in the art of manipulating the media. He was even better at it than Rodgers.

Alou was never to blame. If the team was playing well, it was his doing. If things weren't going well, it was because the front office didn't provide the players he needed. He often criticized both Beattie and me. More often than not, he was wrong. We agreed to live with it given his value and qualities as a manager. But in September 1998, he crossed the line.

At the end of the season, Kevin Malone, the former Expos' general manager now with the Los Angeles Dodgers, told the media he'd love to hire Alou to manage his club. In my opinion, that statement to the press was nothing short of tampering. But Alou didn't seem to be interested. His wife revealed to Bertrand Raymond of the *Journal de Montréal* that for her husband "integrity was sacred." He had a year remaining on his contract, and he intended to remain with the Expos, even if he and Malone had gotten along well when they'd worked together in Montreal.

One day Beattie came to see me in my office and told me he wanted to sound out Alou, to explain to him that we'd like to keep him as manager—not only for that year but also for several years to come. "No problem," I replied. "Go to it." If Beattie felt the need to reassure Alou, it was because of the smear campaign going on in the newspapers. We wanted to keep Felipe, but given the current craziness we didn't want him to think he was forbidden from going elsewhere, if that was what he wanted.

Beattie met with Alou in New York. Essentially, our position was that we wanted Felipe to stay in Montreal; we were even prepared to grant him an immediate contract extension. On the other hand, if he wanted out because of the uncertainty surrounding the team, we wouldn't stand in his way. Beattie was acting in good faith, out of respect for the man and without ulterior motives.

But Alou interpreted the message the opposite way. He said

he'd gotten the impression Beattie was inviting him to leave. The truth was Alou wanted to abandon ship but didn't want to bear the brunt of that decision. So he twisted the meaning of Beattie's words. The faith Beattie wanted to demonstrate in him by immediately renewing his contract worked against us.

Felipe's manipulation succeeded perfectly. In fact, the manager laid it on thick: "It reminds me a little of the revolution in the Dominican Republic in 1965," he said, with all the seriousness in the world, to Serge Touchette of the *Journal de Montréal*. "Once the war was over, the generals were forced into exile."

Revolution? Exile? Why not? I tried to mend fences, but it wasn't easy. After discussing the situation with Alou, I asked him to wait before making a final decision about his future with the organization. He agreed. We decided to talk again within 10 days. But I wasn't optimistic. Later I'd admit I had little hope of seeing Felipe change his mind. But I wanted to try. We needed him.

It was an opportunity sent from heaven for the dissidents in the consortium. The neat bit of wrangling accomplished by Felipe allowed Jacques Ménard to once again come to the fore. Coming out of another meeting of the consortium once again conducted in my absence, Ménard told Martin Leclerc of the *Journal de Montréal* "he'd been appointed to get in touch with Felipe Alou to ask him to stay." Leclerc added, quite rightly, "In memory, it was the first time that the Expos' board of directors [sic] publicly declared its intention to bypass Claude Brochu and get directly involved in baseball operations." It wouldn't be the last time.

The other members of the consortium also put in their two cents' worth. Raymond Bachand of the Solidarity Fund was *furious* about learning of the news via the media. One of his colleagues— anonymously, of course—spoke of sabotage. This "anonymous" owner found it scandalous that we were trying to get rid of the Dominican Alou when we'd just signed a $28 million contract with Vladimir Guerrero, a fellow Dominican who barely spoke English.

At the beginning of October, the journalists went searching for the new investors promised by Ménard and his group. Imasco, the tobacco giant, Bombardier, and Loto-Québec all denied any interest. Same thing for Québécor and Téléglobe, then at its peak. Even Charles Bronfman wasn't interested. . . . And Serge Savard declared himself "surprised at the rumours that propelled him to the presidency of the Expos."

The media were waking up a little. In the *Journal de Montréal*, Martin Leclerc asked, "Have we been witness this week to the creation of an artificial craze for the Expos?" To ask the question was to answer it. Leclerc wasn't the only one to cast aspersions on Ménard's statements. In *La Presse*, Philippe Cantin and Denis Arcand shared his scepticism. Réjean Tremblay admitted we were "swimming in troubled waters" with the Expos' shareholders, who were constantly spreading false rumours.

Despite all that, no one rated my chances of survival very high. "While Jacques Ménard mistakes his dreams for reality," Tremblay wrote, "baseball commissioner Bud Selig is sending him a letter where he says, in essence, to calm down, stop making public statements and stop hurting the image of Claude Brochu" (see appendix, letter of September 30, 1998, page 242). Tremblay added, "It's all very well to dream in technicolor, but Ménard forgets one thing: whatever his intentions, they will have to be ratified by Major League Baseball." A copy of the infamous letter was leaked to Radio-Canada and *La Presse*.

Despite the bad faith displayed by Ménard and his group over those few days, both the partners and the media judged Selig's interference inopportune. As with the visit of National League president Leonard Coleman, Major League Baseball simply wanted to clear things up with the consortium.

But I hoped Selig would get even more involved. I contacted him at his office in Milwaukee. "Listen, Bud, I'd like you to come to Montreal to explain to Lucien Bouchard why the new stadium is so important," I told him. As commissioner of Major League Baseball, Selig might be able to change the premier's mind. It was a last-ditch solution. It wouldn't be the first time Selig intervened with political authorities. He did it all the time. He met with governors, mayors. It was his role as commissioner.

On October 5, I greeted Selig and his legal counsel, Bob DuPuy, at Dorval Airport. My driver, Robert Laird, drove the three of us to Jacques Ménard's offices at Hydro-Québec, where we waited for the premier—for an hour. Selig paced the room. He obviously was losing patience. Finally, we were informed Bouchard was ready to meet with us.

We all packed into the elevator. Laird pushed the button for the 12th floor. Suddenly, sharply, the lights flickered, and the elevator shuddered to a halt. What was happening? A power failure at the Hydro-Québec headquarters? How ironic.

Laird then pushed the button to open the doors. Nothing. He decided to take the situation in hand. Bracing himself against one of the walls of the elevator, he tried to separate the door panels. After some effort, the doors opened. We then discovered we were stuck between two floors. After Laird managed to widen the opening, the five of us, one after another, jumped down to the lower floor. We were safe and sound if a little dishevelled.

Bouchard didn't appear to hold that against us when he and advisor Jean-Roch Boivin finally met with us. I had the impression I was attending a repeat performance of my first meeting with the premier, but this time Selig was the one pleading our case. And very well, in fact. He explained in simple but concrete terms the industry trends, the emergence of new baseball parks in several American cities. He added Montreal would have to follow that trend if we wanted to keep the Expos for many years.

"Quebecers have no interest in baseball," Boivin said at one point.

"Not true," I replied. "They have been great fans for close to 100 years. It is the professional sport that attracts the most people. . . ." I didn't care at all for Boivin's tone or his statements. The advisor was literally getting on my nerves.

A little later, Boivin went back on the attack. "The Expos don't have a solid fan base. The proof? The radio and television ratings are weak. . . ."

I was having more and more trouble keeping my cool. "That is also false," I replied. "More than a million Quebecers listen to the Expos on the radio every week. And the team is also very popular on television. . . ."

Later Boivin went on a second offensive: "Baseball is not part of the Québécois culture. . . ."

This time I could no longer contain myself. *"Cut the bullshit!"*

The premier was insulted. "Mr. Brochu, that type of language is completely unacceptable. And as far as the new stadium is concerned, my government's answer remains the same: we will not make the funds available. That's final." He added, "Go back and do your homework. Revise your business plan."

"Could you be more specific?" I asked. "Could you give us some indication of what you expect? Tell me what you want."

But Bouchard refused to answer. It was clear to me he had other priorities, and I began to understand better the game being played as well as the role of some of the frustrated partners in whatever had pushed Bouchard to turn me down.

While Selig was in Montreal, he publicly reaffirmed his support for me. His intervention on my behalf was coldly received by the media. The commissioner was accused of coming to play in our own backyard, of coming to my rescue and trying to show the "locals" how to run their team. But coming to the aid of clubs was precisely his role—especially since Selig, through revenue sharing and the revenues from the central fund, provided 80% of the team's revenues. We were surviving only because of this formula, which, admittedly, gave Selig the right to be concerned about the future of the team.

The most comical comment came from the *Journal de Montréal*'s Bertrand Raymond, who stated, in all seriousness, "For a long time, the media has felt used in the saga of the Expos." Raymond pointed the finger at league president Leonard Coleman, with his air of a "pseudo public-relations man"; at Bud Selig, who looked like a "funeral director"; and at Claude Brochu, of course, "who is remarkably at ease when he lies." We were accused of having used the media to push our message.

The partners reacted negatively to Selig's visit. On October 6, less than 24 hours before the meeting of all the members of the consortium—including me—all the bridges were officially burned between the partners and me. "It's our money, it's our team, and we will be the ones to decide what we'll do with it" was on the front page of *La Presse*, which also announced to the world the post-Brochu era had already begun.

Raymond Bachand "officially withdrew" his support. For his part, Pierre Michaud confirmed he and I were no longer speaking. "He prefers to bring in his American friends to keep his job," Bachand said, "instead of talking to his shareholders. Our group has people interested in investing, but with him there it won't happen. Claude Brochu is sinking the project. And he's doing it very well, by the way." François Coutu, the son of Jean Coutu, added, "If the Expos clean house, we'll see if we can give them a hand."

The aggressive attitude of the team's co-owners toward Commissioner Selig showed to what extent they were unaware of the scope of the baseball industry. The partners formed a group cut off from the rest of North America. They were preoccupied with their little corner of the universe and the local problems related to the Expos. They forgot the team was one of 30 links in a very tight chain. The interdependence of these links was crucial to the survival of the industry as a whole, an industry led by Selig. Since the members of the consortium didn't understand his role, it's understandable they resented him, this American who was butting into *their* business in *their* city. Some of the partners didn't shy away from disparaging the commissioner, who, in their eyes, was merely a puppet whose comments didn't affect them in the least.

Under normal circumstances, Selig would quickly have quashed any form of protest from an ownership group. Major League Baseball had succeeded in doing so in the past wherever potentially explosive situations occurred. National League President Len Coleman had ably resolved a difficult situation with owner Marge Schott in Cincinnati and the revolt of certain limited partners against the general partner in Pittsburgh. But in Montreal, for obvious reasons, Selig didn't want to. The Expos were in a foreign city where the language and the culture were far different from those in the United States. If the commissioner's office came forward to warn the partners their unacceptable behaviour toward me would earn them severe fines, or even the placement in trust of their shares of the limited partnership, things would have been different. By letting them bark, Selig allowed the situation to deteriorate.

At the time of these events in Montreal, Major League Baseball's executive was going through a major upheaval. In New York, the commissioner's office was in full expansion mode. New departments were being created, and freshly appointed executives were coming in, which caused some shake-ups in the executive offices. Power struggles within his own organization required Selig to pay close attention to what was going on in New York. Montreal's problem would be resolved in due course, they judged, with the wait-and-see attitude typical of Major League Baseball.

The shareholders' game plan was announced at a press conference. "The refinancing of the new stadium will be a long process that will take several months, putting us after the provincial elections. Once we have done our homework and have raised $50 to $70 million, we will be able, in all serenity, to go back and see the governments with a well-put-together project they will not be able to reject."

Shortly afterward, Ménard said the following to Réjean Tremblay of *La Presse*: "A new business plan, which better conforms to the obligations and responsibilities of the premier, will be accepted by the levels of government." A La Presse canadienne reporter cast doubt on the matter with Raymond Bachand, bringing up the fact Premier Bouchard had clearly closed the door to Selig and me during our meeting. Even the federal government was no longer interested in supporting the project. "The governments said no too early and for the wrong reasons. They said no for now," Bachand said.

For me, the statements from Ménard and Bachand were un-equivocal: the members of the consortium had convinced Bouchard not to commit to the stadium project as long as I was in the picture. The die was cast. I'd resisted as long as I could, but that day everything ended.

CHAPTER 17

I Open the Door

After the second refusal from Premier Bouchard, I was certain the stadium project was truly dead. Too many negative comments were circulating left and right; it was impossible to put up a common front to relaunch the project. I myself didn't think I had the strength to act anymore.

I foresaw only one solution for Major League Baseball: to put the team up for sale. If we didn't find any takers in Montreal, we'd turn toward a foreign buyer or buyers. Those buyers could keep the club here or move it to the United States.

But the other partners would never accept such a solution. Their ambition was obvious. They wanted to assume control and propose their own plan of action. Even if Major League Baseball didn't trust Jacques Ménard and his group, the risks were too high on the legal side to force the sale of the team to outside interests.

In this context, I judged the time had come for me to step aside. On September 30, I sent a letter to the partners explaining the procedure to be followed in the case of the sale or transfer of the team. First, Major League Baseball was awaiting a permanent solution to the situation in Montreal, and that solution must involve a significant increase in the local market revenues. Second, any material change in the ownership structure, specifically any change in the control person, had to accord with the mandatory guidelines established by Major League Baseball. A sale (and change of control) require the approval of Major League Baseball before negotiations can begin and before any public announcement can be made.

If a sale (or change of control) process is authorized, I continued, the Ownership Committee of Major League Baseball is authorized to monitor the negotiations and to work closely with the local control party to assess the adequacy and feasibility of any bid received. The Ownership Committee will ultimately make its recommendations to the entire industry for approval.

There were other conditions. Any new ownership structure, regardless of its legal structure, must have one control person designated to make all the decisions. All prospective purchasers must be financially able not only to make the initial investment but also to meet ongoing obligations. A proper financial plan must be presented. And, of course, Major League Baseball requires a continuing commitment to franchise stability.

A meeting of the consortium concerning this matter was scheduled for October 7. Commissioner Bud Selig wanted it to be cancelled or postponed, but I refused. I'd had enough; I wanted to resolve this situation as soon as possible.

On that day, my team, which included Laurier Carpentier, Richard Le Lay, Vice President of Communications Johanne Héroux, and Communications Advisor Michel Capistran, made their way to the Queen Elizabeth Hotel in Montreal. In a conference room, around a long table, the members of the consortium were waiting for me.

Jacques Ménard spoke first. Prior to the meeting, the continuing partners met to establish their own scenario. The first step was my resignation; Raymond Bachand of the Solidarity Fund would replace me. There'd then be an evaluation of the ball club by experts of their choosing. The third and final step was to offer me 7.62% of the value of my shares in the club, net of the accumulated debt.

Obviously, I refused this offer. I wouldn't allow those who'd vowed to bring me down establish the value of my shares. I reminded the partners of the procedure set out in my letter. But it flew 100 feet over their heads.

They saw themselves in the tiny kingdom of the Quebec business world, where they ruled. They thought we could settle this matter among ourselves without involving Major League Baseball. I quickly brought them back to reality. Essentially, we were asking three things of them: find new investors to refinance the club, put together a business plan guaranteeing the Expos would remain in Montreal in the long term, and prepare a stadium plan that would meet the requirements set out by Major League Baseball.

Pierre Michaud lost his temper, becoming very aggressive in his words: "We don't want to have anything to do with you. Get lost! To hell with what the commissioner of baseball wants! He's not the king, he's not going to tell us what to do. We're the ones who will decide what we want to do." Fortunately, tempers cooled, and the partners finally accepted my proposal, approved by the commissioner. Had they not, there would have been an impasse. And the media were waiting in an adjoining room.

The pressure was on my partners, not on me. I then assured them of my complete collaboration and that of my management staff. I promised to run the team in a responsible fashion. I even made a concession. Major League Baseball had proposed a transition period of 60 days. The consortium preferred 150 days. I accepted. The next day, Bud Selig was informed and was opposed to that time frame.

Raymond Bachand turned to Johanne Héroux, introduced himself as her new boss, and asked her to draft a press release. Several of the partners had press attachés or private advisors with them, but none of those public relations people wanted to write the release; nor did they want to organize and oversee the press conference. Héroux and Michel Capistran took the matter in hand.

In the next room, a horde of reporters awaited the results of the deliberations. Several television networks would broadcast the press conference live, and the members of the print media, all the people who'd been hounding me for weeks, had come to attend my funeral.

Gathered in the Queen Elizabeth Hotel kitchens, the continuing partners waited to enter stage left. Capistran said to me, referring to the members of the consortium, "They look like a band of gladiators awaiting the signal to burst into the arena, ready to battle the journalists to the death."

The curtains behind the stage opened, and I appeared. Standing behind the lectern with the media in front of me, my throat parched, I explained my decision to withdraw from the consortium. The words barely came out. I choked once, twice. I desperately wanted a glass of water, but there wasn't one nearby. Someone got one for me.

I was the man whom many people hated so much. But I wasn't the monster many took great pleasure in describing. The stadium project wasn't put together for the money. And my dearest hope—that the team would stay in Montreal—was hardly about money either.

I was completely lost. I wanted the stadium project to become a reality, and I hoped to continue to devote my professional life to the Expos even if I'd lost all confidence in my associates. It was madness on my part. I recognize today I was set up by a bad group of partners. I would never have been able to get out of the situation. My shares in the team would have been frozen. I might have lost everything. . . . But at that point, I told myself I'd resolve all those problems later.

That day, at the Queen Elizabeth Hotel, I didn't have enough hindsight to reflect on all of that. My voice still choked with emotion, I explained I'd remain in place to take care of the team's day-to-day operations during the 150-day transition period. I also mentioned I wouldn't be part of any new consortium. I no longer wanted to be associated with these businessmen. Their hateful behaviour had led me to hate them. They'd also managed to destroy a marvellous organization. I already knew, deep down, that they'd fail miserably in trying to rebuild it.

At the other end of the city, while I concluded my remarks, my beloved wife, Michelle, cried as though her heart would break, all alone in the living room of our apartment. All the efforts her husband had made for nearly 10 years to ensure the survival of the

Expos had been for naught. She cried because she was both sad and angry. For Michelle, the unfair manner in which I'd been treated was unheard of. For those men to attack her husband, an honest man of integrity, was unacceptable. She knew my only goal was to see the Expos succeed in Montreal. Around me, up on the same stage, were arrogant men, manipulators, full of self-importance. Men whom she hated.

And then it was over. I fell silent and left the room without answering any questions from reporters. What purpose would that have served? Everyone was euphoric. My departure meant the rebirth of the Expos!

The reporters then scrummed the hero of the day, Jacques Ménard, who informed them he and his relaunch committee partners would continue to work, during this transition period, on drawing up a plan to attract new investors, finance the stadium, and ensure the Expos' survival in Montreal. As usual, Ménard didn't waste an opportunity to fire off a few pithy quotes. "We will succeed," he told reporters. "Why? It's a bad habit we have to succeed in whatever we undertake." And "The word *failure* is most definitely not in our vocabulary." Words that would haunt Ménard for years to come.

Everyone wanted to believe him. André Rousseau of the *Journal de Montréal* stated Ménard "inspired confidence," especially because he answered questions with a "nice self-assurance." Marshall McLuhan was right: "the medium is the message." Philippe Cantin of *La Presse* was more perceptive. About Ménard, who boasted that the shareholders succeeded in anything they undertook, he wrote, "Claude Brochu could certainly attest to that today. The operation aimed at relieving him of his duties and making him responsible, in the court of public opinion, for the existing stalemate was in fact a tremendous success."

I immediately headed home to be with Michelle; I was worried about her. That night I received a much-appreciated call from Brian Mulroney, and we talked about my situation. He'd also lived through some painful moments with the media, and what he told me was highly encouraging. "Claude, at the end of the day, like me, you will come out of this vindicated."

The following day, I gathered my permanent staff for a breakfast at Olympic Stadium. This whole affair had been very painful for the employees. They no longer knew what to do. They were worried about their jobs, not really knowing if they could believe Ménard's promises. The goal of the meeting was obviously to reassure the employees about their positions with the organization during the transition period and in the long term. I'd effectively remain their boss until the end of the transition period. There would be no other boss; it would be business as usual.

Then I took a few days off. I needed a rest after the trying weeks I'd just lived through. In the plane that took Michelle and me to Florida, I was overcome by the exhaustion of the past few days. It was up to the relaunch committee now to show what it could do.

I was very disappointed, of course. Personal attacks I could handle. In the army, I'd lived through situations far more perilous than a smear campaign. That experience helped me to put all this into perspective. In the end, they were only words. Even if they are cruel and unfair, words don't kill. What saddened me most was the end of my dream.

I knew Ménard and his group would get nowhere. I'd gotten to know them. Since we purchased the club in the early 1990s, they'd done nothing but talk and promise the moon. In every tight situation, I hadn't been able to count on them. Now they could no longer use me as an excuse. Sooner or later, as Bud Selig predicted, they'd begin to argue again, tell each other off, and make a mess of things. With these men in the picture, the Expos could only sink to even lower depths.

But we had to give them a chance. The first problem the relaunch committee had to tackle was Felipe Alou, who was about to sign a contract with the Los Angeles Dodgers.

CHAPTER 18

The Keystone Kops in Action

Before leaving for Florida, I met with Jim Beattie to discuss the Felipe Alou situation. My general manager was profoundly troubled by this whole affair. Honest, conscientious, Beattie never understood how Alou could have doubted his good faith. At the press conference where he explained his side of the story, he was unable to hold back his tears, the situation had so shattered him.

At this point, Alou was at his home in Lake Worth, Florida, and had been negotiating with the Dodgers ever since we'd given him permission to do so. If we wanted to keep him, we had to act now. Beattie had come to Florida to discuss the situation with his manager while I was on vacation.

I authorized Jim to match the salary the Dodgers were offering—but no more than that. In our eyes, Alou was hardly the idol the public and reporters made him out to be. Since he'd demonstrated his desire to leave the team, I'd discussed it with him and reminded him we still wanted him to stay. I'd suggested he let his heart dictate his choice.

For their part, the partners wanted Alou to remain in Montreal —at any cost. At the October 7 meeting, they'd offered to help me convince Alou to stay. Jacques Ménard even appealed to Monsignor Jean-Claude Turcotte, the archbishop of Montreal, whom he knew through the diocese's fund-raising campaigns. Monsignor Turcotte phoned Alou in Florida to ask him not to abandon the Expos.

Now the members of the consortium wanted to send Ménard and Mark Routtenberg to Lake Worth to support Beattie's efforts. I agreed, but it was understood they'd be there to appease him, to reiterate how much we needed him, to tell him how valuable he was to the team. I didn't for an instant imagine they intended to negotiate with him.

The following Monday, still in Florida, I received a call from Bud Selig. The commissioner was furious. "What the hell is going on?"

What *was* going on? I'd never heard him in such a state.

"You gave $6 million to Alou!"

"What?"

"Two million a year. I talked to the president of the Dodgers. They were ready to give him a million a year for three years. You offered him twice that! Are you crazy?"

"Let me get to the bottom of this story, Bud, and I'll call you back," I said. "This isn't how it's going to go, I assure you."

I understood the commissioner's anger. The Expos, the poorest team in Major League Baseball, were 80% financed by the other clubs. That meant 80% of Alou's salary would be paid by money coming directly from Major League Baseball's coffers. Despite this precarious situation, we'd be treating ourselves to one of the two highest-paid managers in the majors (along with Jim Leyland of the Colorado Rockies). How would the other clubs react? How much money would other managers demand as a result of a move that threatened to become a reference point in future negotiations?

The initiative by Ménard and Routtenberg was classic stupidity, an ill-considered act that would get all of the other owners on our backs. They'd driven up the bidding by bidding against themselves.

As soon as I hung up with Selig, I called Beattie, who uncomfortably confirmed the deal. "Through Routtenberg, the partners authorized me to go up to $2 million," he said.

"That is sheer madness."

"Routtenberg promised him something else too," Beattie continued.

I closed my eyes. I expected the worst.

"In the name of the consortium, he guaranteed Felipe the new stadium would be built and the payroll would be increased so we could put our hands on quality free agents."

Disaster. Routtenberg and the others had no way of guaranteeing they could keep this promise. And we didn't have the means to pay $6 million to our manager.

When I hung up the phone, I leaned back in my chair. The relaunch committee's first blunder was a monumental one, but Ménard and Routtenberg would come off as champion negotiators. They'd managed to keep Alou, the media would proclaim. But at what cost? And on what conditions? Obviously, Ménard and Routtenberg didn't live on the same planet as the other Major League Baseball executives.

To the media, Alou admitted he was astounded; the club "had made an offer beyond his expectations." According to Jack Todd of the Montreal *Gazette*, while Beattie and Routtenberg were negotiating with Alou in his home, Kevin Malone and Dodgers president Bob Graziano were driving around the block in a rental car, awaiting his decision.

Bertrand Raymond of the *Journal de Montréal* added more. To explain the choice of Routtenberg as negotiator, Raymond wrote, "Routtenberg had formed a nice friendship with Alou. And that card was played; they told themselves the manager surely would listen to what Routtenberg had to tell him." Raymond added, "The selfless gesture of Jacques Ménard is worthy of mention. He very easily could have given himself the starring role. . . . Since the Expos have a lot of money to offer Alou, he could have played the hero by returning from Florida with the agreement from the manager they coveted." And there was more. "When they don't have somebody jamming something in their spokes, these people seem able to pedal quite well, wouldn't you say?"

Give me a break! While the praise for Ménard and Routtenberg continued, I had to deal with the consequences of their decision.

Selig was so angry he threatened to void the contract, and he had the power to do it. I begged him not to because Beattie had acted within the framework of his responsibilities in proposing the contract to Alou. We'd committed an irresponsible act, but we couldn't go back on our word. Selig accepted my argument reluctantly but decided to send a task force to Montreal to undertake a detailed analysis of the situation. There was little in the prevailing climate of the club's management that would reassure him.

Bill Bartholomay, chairman of the Ownership Committee and chairman of the Board of Directors of the Atlanta Braves, Tom Ostertag and Bob Kheel, both from Major League Baseball's legal services department, as well as Major League Baseball public relations advisor Len Sanderson, landed in Montreal a few days after the signing of Alou's contract. Selig's emissaries toured the offices, then knocked on the doors of some of the continuing partners. They demanded explanations from Ménard and Routtenberg about Alou's contract. All of a sudden, the two became very humble. They claimed to have been nothing more than observers; it was Beattie who'd made all the decisions. They'd simply been advisors to him.

The task force's oral report confirmed what Selig already suspected. From all appearances, the consortium was made up of irresponsible men who had no clue about the impact of their actions and knew nothing about the business of professional baseball. Without a doubt, the team's relaunch plan was doomed.

From that moment on, I asked Beattie to take no action without my permission. He kept his word. The partners never again interfered in purely baseball-related decisions.

During the summer of 1998, I retained the services of Jacques Ménard and Nesbitt Burns, as well as RBC Dominion Securities, to help prepare various financial options related to the identification of potential sources of government revenue that could be used to help fund the new ballpark. Which they did, but not very well. I never saw their report, but we received a bill for $1 million.

Ménard and Nesbitt Burns now had to approach new investors and sell shares worth $150 million in the new partnership. In return, Ménard and Nesbitt Burns received a monthly remuneration, along with the possibility of a $2 million commission if they were successful.

According to Ménard, new investors had come forward. Loto-Québec was mentioned. Laurent Pépin of Provigo even spoke of a list of "wealthy Montrealers judged likely to invest in the Expos." As well, Premier Bouchard was said to be ready now to meet with the Expos' executives and listen to their latest proposals given the "new support" from the business community. Nothing concrete, once again, but everyone wanted to believe Ménard.

Speaking for the continuing partners, Ménard also announced the "death of the Brochu plan" and revealed that discussions between the partners and me had begun about the repurchase of my shares in the consortium. The newspapers even predicted Serge Savard would replace me as the team's top executive.

Just as in 1990, during acquisition of the team from Charles Bronfman, Nesbitt Burns put together a confidential information memorandum to give to potential investors. Normally, this document would require approval from Expos' management. But Laurier Carpentier and the rest of the vice presidents refused to ratify the financial projections prepared by Nesbitt Burns. The memorandum enumerated a long list of risk factors, long enough to make any investor who was the least bit conscientious think twice. Ménard and his team corrected the document several times, but Carpentier was never satisfied. The revenue projections were so unrealistic he refused to be associated with them. After the 18th draft, Carpentier chose to put an end to his involvement.

Without the support of management, Nesbitt Burns nonetheless sent the document to potential investors. The continuing partners decided to go ahead with study committees, as they'd promised the media they'd do upon my departure.

Ménard explained you had to consider the Expos' project, in all its complexity, the way you would a construction site. You had to divide it up. The partners took charge of three major issues: the plans for a new stadium, the refinancing of the team, and the search for a majority partner. "This partner could be the Expos' representative with Major League Baseball, with extensive powers," Ménard declared. "If there is consultation, there won't be a problem."

The Expos' vice presidents and employees participated in these committee meetings to help the partners understand the "business" and attempt to answer their questions. Over the next 12 months— even though I didn't speak with them directly—we communicated, via my lawyer, Pierre-André Themens of Goodman, Phillips and Vineberg, and their lawyer, Gérard Coulombe of Monet, Desjardins, Ducharme. Both men did extraordinary work to help the relaunch committee.

The committees responsible for each of those three issues, which operated with input from team management, never hired a competent advisor to guide them through this process. Quite incredible. A $150 million deal, and they did it on their own. As well, the members of the consortium were involved on only a part-time basis given their other jobs.

The confusion was even greater in their relationship with Major League Baseball. Because of their gaffe during the renewal of Felipe Alou's contract, and their overall behaviour, Ménard and his group lost all credibility with Bud Selig and the owners. Their contact was limited to discussions with Paul Beeston and Bob DuPuy, respectively President of Major League Baseball and Vice President of Major League Baseball's legal department.

Selig avoided Ménard as much as possible. The two men spoke only on rare occasions, partly because Ménard's verbosity got on the commissioner's nerves. As Selig reportedly loved to say, if Ménard were paid by the word, he'd be richer than Charles Bronfman! When Ménard called Major League Baseball headquarters in New York, as part of a conference call, Beeston, DuPuy, and league president Leonard Coleman would listen to his interminable monologues while following a ball game on television.

From my office at Olympic Stadium, I watched the relaunch committee in action. They reminded me of the Keystone Kops, those comic silent-movie characters, the white-helmeted constables who were always chasing someone, running left and right, incapable of collaring the criminals. Knowing nothing of the current practices in the baseball industry, Ménard, Routtenberg, and the others made nice speeches, tried to impress people, but convinced no one— except, of course, the many reporters who swallowed whole everything fed to them.

In this context, it was hardly surprising new investors were slow to come forward. Where were the companies, according to Ménard and friends, that were waiting only for my departure to commit to the rebirth of the team? Routtenberg declared to the media, "Things are moving at a snail's pace, and it's frustrating, but they're moving in the right direction. We will have good news to announce by Christmas."

What was going on? What was wrong? And whose fault was it? Mine, obviously. Even though I was out of the way, I was supposedly scaring off potential investors. "Brochu is blocking everything," declared Martin Leclerc of the *Journal de Montréal*. Pierre Michaud of Provigo revealed that "many are waiting to find out how much Brochu's departure will cost before they entertain the possibility of taking out their chequebooks." Utter nonsense.

On November 19, 1998, things began to move. Loblaws, an Ontario-based supermarket chain, announced it would invest $10 million in the new partnership as part of its acquisition of Provigo, itself a partner in the consortium. Michaud, chairman of the board of Provigo, revealed this information during Jean Lapierre's program on radio station CKAC. During the negotiations with Loblaws, Michaud had discussed the Expos with the Ontario supermarket chain's executives and apparently had convinced them not only to maintain Provigo's share of the team but also to kick in an extra $10 million. There was only one condition: I had to be removed.

When I'd agreed to step aside, we'd all agreed on the procedure to be followed. I'd continue to run the day-to-day operations of the team while the continuing partners found new investors and put together a new business plan for the team and construction of Labatt Park. They had all the freedom to do what they wanted, and it was clear to everyone I'd leave my job as soon as their mandate was completed. I always told them that, when everything was in place to ensure the Expos would stay in Montreal for the next 20 years, I'd step aside. That was the information I was waiting for. Staying on had nothing to do with money.

The continuing partners' strategy was clear. Unable to find new investors and complete their business plan, they still needed me as a scapegoat. By casting the blame on me once again, they deflected media attention away from what they were doing—or, more accurately, what they weren't doing.

In mid-December, Ménard stated everything was going well. To Michel Blanchard of *La Presse*, he declared himself "satisfied with the work accomplished to this point." Only 100 days remained in the 150-day transition period prescribed for the relaunching of the team, but Ménard added, "We should be in a position to settle the Claude Brochu situation between Christmas and mid-January." (He was to come and see me in Florida to discuss it. He never got in touch with me.) Added Ménard, "We should be ready to meet with the various levels of government by the end of February or the beginning of March. In the meantime, we continue to work on the recapitalization of the team and the sale of seats and corporate boxes in our new stadium." He concluded by saying, "I sense great interest."

It was true things were taking shape. After Jean Coutu, after Loblaws, another investor came forward: Stephen Bronfman. Charles Bronfman's son said he was prepared to contribute $10 million to the relaunch plan. Ménard proposed instead that he contribute $25 million and become president of the team. Stephen didn't see himself in such a major role; what interested him about the Expos was the success of the relaunch committee—if only to remain faithful to his father's legacy. As well, the younger Bronfman believed the Expos were important to Montreal's economy.

Pierre Michaud of Provigo tried to interest Sam Eltes of Silver Star Mercedes, who over the years had always been a friend of the Expos. Michaud asked him to invest $5 million. His answer? "All right, I'll put in $5 million of my personal money, if you do the same!" Michaud was quite prepared to invest other people's money, but in no way would he risk his own. He refused the counteroffer, and Eltes turned down the proposal.

The Keystone Kops also wasted no time in piling up blunders in the development of the new stadium. Laurier Carpentier, who'd continued to work on the stadium project after my withdrawal, sounded the alarm before it was too late (see appendix, letter dated January 20, 1999, page 243). According to Carpentier, in their eagerness to break ground as soon as possible, the partners were prepared to run dangerous risks. Since they had to deliver a turn-key stadium under a tight deadline and on a restricted budget (we were now talking about $150 million to $180 million instead of the original $250 million), no doubt the contractor would demand financial escape clauses in the contract. Carpentier warned the continuing partners about the cost overruns that could result from such an approach. And the reduced cost could result in a stadium of lesser scope and inferior quality and, consequently, force them to make unacceptable compromises in terms of its operation, use, or aesthetics.

As well, sensitive to the complaints of various lobby groups calling for subsidized housing in that sector of Montreal, city authorities asked the consortium for permission to put up a residential building between the future stadium and the buildings located on the other side of de la Montagne. This compromise would completely change the architectural aspect of the ballpark and significantly reduce the available space. As it was, the site was already a little small for the stadium. A tremendous error, according to Carpentier. If the consortium accepted the city's proposal before a detailed plan had even been presented, the group would lose all leverage with the municipal authorities. The result would be that the city's requirements, before and during construction, would create delays and additional costs. Unfortunately, in their quest to please everyone and avoid any confrontation (the City of Montreal was a co-owner of the team), the partners agreed to the city's suggestion.

As well, still according to Carpentier, the seat-licence plan no longer held water. After being disparaged by the partners, the plan, which I'd originally put together, had been revamped. The content remained the same except for a few major details.

In the initial proposal, acquisition of a licence for a seat or a corporate box gave the investor the right to buy a season ticket for that seat or box for subsequent seasons. Only the revenue culled from the sale of licences would be put toward construction of the stadium. With the new plan, it was still possible for a company to commit in this way, but it could also elect to buy only season tickets—which would be a lot cheaper. According to Carpentier, we could expect that most companies, not wanting to take a risk, would choose the latter approach. The ball club would then be short of funds needed for construction.

Finally, Carpentier brought up the question of players' salaries. By increasing the payroll to 87% of the Major League Baseball average (compared with the current 50%), the continuing partners committed to offering the fans a winning team—one that would have a chance of making regular postseason appearances. Carpentier said the stadium would have to be filled to 86% of its capacity—even during April, May, and September—to generate sufficient revenue to meet that increased payroll. He doubted fans were prepared to brave the elements in the spring and fall even in a new stadium. By reducing the costs related to construction of the stadium, the consortium increased the risk there'd be fewer people who'd come to see the team play.

Carpentier's conclusion was clear. From those data, baseball had no future in Montreal. The compromises made in construction of the stadium, the changes in the seat-licence plan, and the unrealistic expectations of the continuing partners threatened the success of the effort. Carpentier therefore handed the consortium his resignation. He'd leave a few months later.

The members of the consortium were in shock. Carpentier's report laid out the situation in precise terms, but they refused to take it seriously. Some of the partners believed Carpentier had simply taken down my dictation. To have contemplated that possibility for a second was not to know Carpentier, a man of integrity and honesty. But, remember, I had only one objective: to sabotage their efforts.

The partners wanted to ask Ernst & Young to study the viability of professional baseball in Montreal. It was a good idea. But that study would never see the light of day.

CHAPTER 19

Public Enemy Number One

On February 4, 1999, Bob DuPuy of Major League Baseball's legal department wrote to Jacques Ménard and me. "We are disappointed that there appears to be no progress with respect to government commitment, the zoning and municipal tax issues so critical to the development of the stadium have not gotten closer to resolution, the new investor base is not yet committed nor is it at this point particularly expansive, the revised stadium concepts have not yet been reviewed and we do not know if they will be acceptable or adequate to you or to Baseball . . ." (see appendix, letter dated February 4, 1999, page 250).

DuPuy had reason for concern. Unable to find the millions necessary for the relaunch of the team, unable to count on a commitment from any level of government, the continuing partners were going in circles. It was obvious in the current context that neither Quebec City nor Ottawa wanted to take a stand on the issue. The support from the business community was weakening day by day, and the slapdash investment prospectus, the one Laurier Carpentier had refused to sign off on, wasn't likely to attract serious investors.

At the commissioner's offices in New York, executives were increasingly getting the impression some of the partners were running out of gas and perhaps searching for a way out. Some of them would surely be amenable to putting the team up for sale. The only reasonable solution in the current context was to hand the team to American buyers and move the franchise to the United States. But Ménard was "condemned to succeed," as he put it. He'd so committed himself during that press conference at the Queen Elizabeth Hotel that he couldn't give up now, not so soon.

As agreed, I continued to run the team without interference, with the notable exception of Felipe Alou's contract renewal. Now Mark Routtenberg tried to force me to increase the payroll. I refused.

So again the continuing partners tried to push me aside. They asked me if I'd allow a representative from the partnership to oversee my work. They also wanted to meddle in the day-to-day operations and to set up shop in our offices. Out of the question, I said. I didn't want this Tower of Babel anywhere near us. Let them continue with their mission of finding investors; let them improve their plans for refinancing the team and the new stadium. They had their hands full without interfering in the management of the team and throwing my staff into a panic, just by their presence.

Without a doubt, the continuing partners were headed straight toward disaster. Having lost all credibility with Major League Baseball, without the support of the public, the governments, and the business world, they once again fell back on their usual game plan: going to war with me. Ménard and his group had undoubtedly convinced themselves yet again that I was in cahoots with Major League Baseball. To justify an eventual failure, they could always proclaim loudly that they'd done their best but that Selig and I had sabotaged their efforts.

The partners had convinced journalists I had only one objective from the start: making money, to the detriment of the team's shareholders. Over the years, I'd deliberately weakened the team by holding fire sales. Hadn't Felipe Alou admitted in 1993 I didn't want to win because I didn't want to disturb the broad outlines of my plan? I'd denigrated Olympic Stadium to alienate the public. Perhaps I was even responsible for the concrete beam collapsing, therefore justifying my plans for a new stadium, a new white elephant, and dragging along honest but naïve businessmen who were taken in from beginning to end. Now, his "plan" having succeeded, Machiavelli was on his way to the bank.

Bertrand Raymond of the *Journal de Montréal* sounded the charge. "We were had by Brochu. Shareholders outmanoeuvred, fans duped, and media manipulated." He called me "underhanded" before adding there was no better word to describe my diabolical plot. The headline from colleague Yvon Pedneault's article was even more virulent: "A con! From a majority partner who was hungry, manipulative, dangerous."

The offensive intensified on February 18, 1999, at downtown Complexe Desjardins, as part of a press conference called by the relaunch committee to update the search for new investors and the stadium financing issue. It was a mega press conference—something the committee was making a habit of—broadcast live on Montreal radio and television stations. Front and centre on the stage was Jacques Ménard, flanked by Jocelyn Proteau, Pierre Michaud, Raymond Bachand, and Mark Routtenberg. After announcing that American Jeffrey Loria, who wasn't present, was ready to invest $70 million in the team and that a dozen anonymous investors would put in $50 million, Ménard and his group descended on public enemy number one—me—with renewed vehemence for almost an hour on live television and radio.

"Be a good citizen, Claude. Clear the way . . ." was the mantra repeated by one businessman after another, downcast one and all, in an overly dramatic tone of voice. You'd have thought their very survival was at stake. "If we don't come to terms with him in the next few weeks, we might have to call you here again to tell you we're throwing in the towel," said Proteau, full of pathos. Once again they heaped scorn on me; I was the only one to blame for the Expos' misfortunes. The message was clear enough, but Michaud reiterated it to make sure everyone understood: "We need Claude Brochu out of here."

I watched the press conference in my office. What I heard didn't surprise me. Almost no one seemed to cast doubt on the outrageous remarks spouted by Ménard and the other partners.

Richard Labbé of *La Presse* wrote, "The shareholders' message was crystal clear: it was impossible to make progress with the Expos in Montreal as long as Claude Brochu remained the organization's main leader." Martin Leclerc of the *Journal de Montréal* quoted Ménard. "In addition to having hurt the franchise, Claude Brochu never kept his word." And, Leclerc added, "In living memory, never have we ever witnessed such a settling of accounts, in public, by representatives from the business world."

The English-language reporters weren't left behind. David Johnston of the Montreal *Gazette* reported Routtenberg's words without batting an eyelash. "Routtenberg said the other Expos owners want to replace Brochu because he has made a series of bad executive decisions," Johnston wrote. He quoted Routtenberg as saying I should have vetoed a 1993 transfer of the money-rich and therefore player-rich Atlanta Braves into the same division as the Expos. That I put too much faith in a revenue-sharing deal that took effect in 1996. That I'd managed ultraconservatively without taking any risks. "As a result of this type of management, he [Brochu] has continuously traded down until we were off the map with product and entertainment. He destroyed all our credibility and support from fans and sponsors by tearing down the team every time it reached a pinnacle." All this according to Routtenberg.

Whether radio or television reporters, commentators, analysts, or even newspaper columnists, nearly everyone accepted the opinions put forth by the relaunch committee as gospel. Ménard and his group managed to convince everyone I was a traitor, a sellout, even a criminal who had only my own interests at heart. On CKAC, Réjean Tremblay gave me a new nickname, a variation of my last name: Crochu, meaning "crooked." Without a doubt, it wasn't the greatest day in the history of Quebec journalism.

On the other hand, the continuing partners who'd come to the Expos' rescue had things well in hand. They were in control of the situation and would somehow manage to fix the mistakes—deliberate mistakes, they claimed—I'd made.

What struck me the most in watching that press conference was the lack of class of these five individuals on the stage. The leaders of the business community were behaving like village roosters.

Why didn't I react to these attacks? I couldn't. Whatever I said, I'd have taken a beating the following day. At the club's training camp in Florida, I said only this to Pierre Ladouceur of *La Presse*: "During the October 7 press conference, I made a commitment not to make any statements during the 150-day transition period, so as to allow the shareholders complete latitude to proceed with their relaunch plan."

But these attacks wounded me deeply. Especially when I was accused of having plotted with Bud Selig and National League president Leonard Coleman to take the ball club out of town—a strategy that apparently went back five years. Or when I was accused of negotiating the team's move to Washington, DC, so I could remain club president. All of that was false.

Réjean Tremblay of *La Presse* refused to believe I was sincere. "It's almost indecent to have to listen to that," he wrote, indignant. "Thankfully, Claude Brochu cannot manage to perfectly control his body language when he lies."

Thanks to the collusion of some journalists who were pushing the image of me as a diabolical fiend, Ménard and his group had managed to convince the public they weren't responsible for the lack of progress in the refinancing of the team and the new stadium.

Philippe Cantin of *La Presse* understood the game being played by the partners, who were acting in a way that would result in my being blamed if the project were aborted. According to Cantin, Ménard and his group were acting as though they didn't want the initiative to succeed. He deplored the lack of leadership in the consortium. And he found their sudden interest in baseball suspicious. "It wasn't so long ago," Cantin wrote, "that Mr. Roberge rejected the idea of building a downtown stadium; Provigo, under the reign of Pierre Michaud, has never participated in any marketing campaign on behalf of the Expos; and when the organization borrowed a large sum after the 1994 strike, it was a New York bank that provided the money, not the Caisses Populaires Desjardins."

The 150-day deadline was looming, and the relaunch committee's promises had yet to be fulfilled. The continuing partners had other things to do. As Cantin revealed, over the previous months Ménard had attended the Davos summit in Switzerland as chairman of the board of Hydro-Québec. Michaud spent the fall selling Provigo to Loblaws, while Proteau dealt with a management restructuring at Desjardins. For his part, Roberge was hoping to open a new store downtown. Not surprising, then, that the work hadn't been done.

Ménard then asked Major League Baseball for an open-ended extension of the deadline, set to expire on March 6. He was refused. Extension or not, Major League Baseball was convinced Ménard and his group couldn't bring their plans to fruition. No progress had been made in terms of the relaunch plan. As well, the Bouchard government continued its public opposition to providing assistance for the new stadium.

In a letter sent to Ménard, Bob DuPuy didn't shy away from taking issue with some of the statements Ménard had made at the February 18 press conference (see appendix, letter dated February 25, 1999, page 253). Contrary to what had been claimed, Major League Baseball had never "received a written understanding from Jeffrey Loria" regarding his potential investment in the team. It had never supported a new control person. As well, DuPuy was unhappy about the disparaging comments that had been made about me.

Livid at having been identified by Major League Baseball as partly responsible for the lack of progress in the relaunch of the Expos, Premier Bouchard found the position taken by Bud Selig and Major League Baseball unpleasant and ill mannered. Bouchard even participated in the smear campaign against me. "I don't have to say anything more about Mr. Brochu than has already been said by his colleagues. That's already quite a bit," he told reporters. Bouchard's error was to accept out of hand what the partners were proposing: a reduced-cost project that didn't include my involvement. By not taking the time to comprehensively analyse the initial project submitted to him, by refusing to listen seriously to what

I had to say, the premier had contributed to the chaos in which the partnership was now mired.

Criticized by some reporters for offending the sensibilities of Major League Baseball by attacking me so ferociously, snubbed by Major League Baseball executives who pretty much considered him a liar, Ménard resorted to the tactic that had worked so well in the past: denigrating me. Following an interview of Ménard by CKAC's Ron Fournier, Réjean Tremblay of *La Presse* wrote there could be no doubt of "the complicity and duplicity of Claude Brochu and his sidekicks in Commissioner Bud Selig's office." He spoke of a "plan to crush the consortium." Ménard *confirmed* Selig and I had concocted a plan to move the Expos to Washington, DC. "They can push us to the brink of the abyss," Ménard added, "but we refuse to give up. We want to succeed, but, when there are people on the other side of the fence who don't want us to, it's much more difficult." Quoting Ménard, Tremblay wrote, "Claude Brochu and Major League Baseball are trying to commit robbery." Worse, I was not only a thief but a murderer as well. "It is now certain that Claude Brochu is doing his utmost to kill the Expos," Tremblay added.

A move to Washington, Machiavellian plots. . . . The truth was much simpler than that. Major League Baseball had refused to extend the deadline (see appendix, letter dated March 17, 1999, page 255) because it had no confidence in Ménard and his group. Not to mention the members of the consortium couldn't have cared less about the procedures regarding the transfer of power. But above all, their attitude was their undoing. Had the partners demonstrated a modicum of civility, Major League Baseball would have agreed to their request for an extension. They were asking the commissioner for favours after denigrating him. It was understandable he sent them packing.

It was a waste of effort. The continuing partners didn't know the first thing about social graces. I can personally attest to that.

With the exception of a few short interviews at the beginning of training camp in Jupiter, I still hadn't delivered my version of events. I hadn't responded to the vicious and personal attacks. At the beginning of March 1999, I thought the time had come to make my point of view known.

CHAPTER 20

The Return of Bernard Landry . . . and Jeffrey Loria

Still in Jupiter, I convened the media for a press conference that would be broadcast via satellite back to Montreal. Three things were bothering me. First, several journalists claimed I'd never invested any of my own money in the Expos. They said that to diminish me, to prove I was a profiteer. One journalist even confided to me he knew it was false, but his bosses wanted him to say it anyway. I reminded them that in 1990 Charles Bronfman lent me $2 million, which I invested in the purchase of the team. I acquired additional shares over the years as I elected to receive shares in the ball club in lieu of annual bonuses.

Second, I vigorously denied the rumour that Commissioner Selig and I secretly intended to move the team to Washington, DC—or any other American city, for that matter. Were that the case, I explained, I would never have battled so fiercely to institute the revenue-sharing program so critical to the ball club's survival. And I certainly wouldn't have invested $6 million of the team's money in the downtown stadium project.

Third, I reminded everyone that the committee headed by Jacques Ménard hadn't fulfilled its mandate and that its relaunch plan was unworkable. No significant new investors had confirmed their participation and the Quebec government was still refusing to commit, although there was some movement on that front.

Following the initiatives of Major League Baseball, the repeated demands from the members of the consortium, and the pressure

199

exerted by sportswriters, Premier Bouchard wanted to move but without committing himself. Mostly, he wanted to get rid of the pressure that was becoming increasingly heavy. Following his categorical no to Jacques Ménard, Bud Selig, and me, the premier was being considered the Expos' gravedigger—the one who'd played right into my hands. Just when we'd given up hope, Bouchard announced he intended to help the Expos at last. He then entrusted the project to . . . Bernard Landry.

Landry wasn't particularly happy to have this dossier dropped back into his lap after it had been taken away in most cavalier fashion seven months earlier, especially because in the interim the entire situation had deteriorated. When Landry's team was talking with my team, the financing plan for the new stadium had made sense. Now everything had been changed and diluted. We were no longer talking about the same project.

Landry asked my government advisor, Richard Le Lay, if the new version of the project had any chance of succeeding. Le Lay's answer was categorical: "In no way," he said. "The numbers didn't hold water; their plan was just a house of cards." Le Lay wasn't the only one to think that; no one in the minister of finance's entourage had confidence in the partnership's initiatives.

During a meeting with the relaunch committee, Landry greeted Pierre Michaud in the elevator. "Ah, the Mr. Michaud who sold Réno-Dépot to the Belgians and Provigo to the Ontarians. And now he wants to save the Expos!"

But Landry had to act; orders from Bouchard were clear. At the end of March, the Quebec government surprised everyone by announcing its plan to contribute $7 to $8 million Canadian a year from the tourism budget. This amount would cover the interest on an eventual $100 million loan for construction of the stadium.

At first glance, the commitment appeared generous. But it was really a risk-free political manoeuvre by the government. Landry's offer came with several firm conditions. The consortium had to find private investors to contribute $125 million, acquire the rights to the chosen building site, and finance half of the construction costs for the new stadium with capital injected by the partners or from the sale of seat licences. These were unworkable conditions given the improvisation and disorganization the consortium had demonstrated to that point. As well, according to the agreement, the partners had to assume the eventual long-term capital costs of stadium repairs and maintenance.

A bad deal. But the members of the consortium had it coming. By sabotaging my initial efforts with the Quebec government, Ménard and the others had let it be known they could do better than I'd been doing. Now they had to prove it. Their backs to the wall, dealing with a modified, ill-conceived project, they had no choice but to accept exacting conditions that reduced their room in which to manoeuvre. This deal would end up being signed. But it would never be implemented.

In April 1999 came more proof of the lack of social grace of the continuing partners. In front of the media, Raymond Bachand of the Solidarity Fund scolded the Expos' marketing department, which, according to him, had been doing a "pitiful" job. Bachand blamed the Expos for insufficiently advertising the appearance in Montreal of St. Louis Cardinals slugger Mark McGwire, who was on the verge of breaking the National League home-run record. As if the Canadiens had to advertise when Wayne Gretzky came to town. . . .

The marketing staff were justifiably furious. Bachand's accusations, made in very public fashion, cast doubt on their competence and dedication. Even those who didn't work in the marketing department felt targeted by Bachand's attack. For good reason there as well. Under difficult circumstances, as the team's public image was suffering (mainly because of the initiatives of Bachand and his partners), management and staff nevertheless continued to support the ball club and did everything they could to ensure the team's success. Bachand had just told them in public they were dragging their heels.

The team's five administrative vice presidents—Laurier Carpentier, Michel Bussière, Johanne Héroux, Claude Delorme, and Richard Morency—responded to Bachand as a group in writing (see appendix, letter dated May 3, 1999, page 257). They denounced his comments. They accused him of "disparaging the product," an accusation often thrown at me by the consortium, as it happened. "Your comments have had a demoralizing impact on every employee," the letter stated. "We were surprised to hear such comments coming from the President of the Solidarity Fund, who is supposed to defend workers, not undermine their credibility."

Other Expos' employees also made their anger known. Vice President of Baseball Operations Bill Stoneman, a star player with the inaugural team in 1969, could no longer put up with the scornful contempt for employees displayed by some members of the consortium. Until that point, Stoneman had stayed out of the internal squabbles that had sullied the team's reputation. But following Bachand's remarks, he'd decided to denounce the attitude of some members of the consortium.

In a letter to Jacques Ménard, Stoneman mostly blamed Jocelyn Proteau, Mark Routtenberg, Pierre Michaud, Paul Roberge, Jean Coutu, and Ménard himself for their relentless criticism and mean-spirited accusations (see appendix, letter dated May 3, 1999, page 259). Stoneman wrote, "Like Felipe Alou, his coaches and our 25 players, those of us who are Expos employees consider ourselves a team. While we are not always right, we always work hard to be right." He continued on, referring to Bachand's remarks. ". . . I'd like someone with any amount of business sense to tell me what possible good can result when an owner (or someone representing an owner) of a company makes public comments that denigrate the company's own employees. . . ."

Stoneman was appalled at the "harmful comments" from Proteau, Routtenberg, Michaud, Roberge, Coutu, and Ménard, appalled that they'd taken turns inciting the media to join them in "a public-relations campaign reminiscent of some of the dirtiest political campaigns in memory, mostly directed at Claude Brochu. . . . Who in your group thinks that such public-relations efforts will help achieve a long-term solution to keep baseball in Montreal?"

Stoneman wondered. "To their credit," he wrote, "those who represent Canadian Pacific, BCE, Télémédia, McClelland & Stewart and Cascades appear to have steered clear of your smear campaign."

Stoneman had no doubt Ménard, Routtenberg, and the others wanted to find someone to blame for their possible failure. "Keep in mind that when you take shots at Claude Brochu, Richard Morency, our marketing employees, or anyone else working for this team, you are shooting at my teammates," Stoneman wrote. "I hope you will understand when I say I resent it. More importantly, I hope you understand that such emotional nonsense is not productive."

While employees were calling into question the initiatives and attitudes of the consortium, Major League Baseball was intensifying the pressure on Ménard and his group. Legal counsel Bob DuPuy asked consultant Bob Starkey of the firm of Arthur Andersen to undertake a detailed study of the stadium plan proposed by the consortium. Since the continuing partners had taken over, three project bids had been submitted by three separate contractors. All three projects had proposed a revised version of my initial plans.

Starkey's conclusions were to be expected. The stadium plans submitted by Ménard's group received C minuses and Ds, while my project had received an A. Starkey was equally strict in grading Ménard's business plan. According to Starkey, the plan was very risky and depended far too heavily on the generosity of the revenue-sharing system. If this system were reduced, the Expos would incur losses. As well, the plan reduced the goal for the seat-licence plan from $75 million to $25 million, which represented a major shortfall for the team to make up.

In terms of the commitment from the government and the new investors, Major League Baseball was hardly reassured, even though Ménard coated his responses with his usual vague answers and clichés. Excerpts from Ménard's correspondence with New York show why: "The government has made it known that it would be open to considerations . . . on condition that we maintain negotiations . . . might be convinced to reevaluate his position . . . presently

we are evaluating the possibilities . . . we are optimistic and some-
what confident . . . we will find something . . . a preliminary
position . . . we are just beginning. . . ." A flood of vague statements completely removed from reality.

Ménard maintained the same attitude with the media. Despite
the serious doubts expressed by Major League Baseball, Ménard
continued to declare everything was rolling along: the plan for
the new stadium was ready, the relaunch plan was efficient and
innovative, the investors were breaking down the door trying to
get in. According to him, the Quebec government was ready to
come on board, the land had been acquired, and the municipal tax
questions had been resolved. But most of all, Ménard concluded,
Major League Baseball would give them all the time they needed
to pull it off. Once again Ménard and his group mistook their
dreams for reality.

This attitude was only harmful. I hailed the commitment of the
Quebec government even if the deal wasn't very advantageous. It
was a step in the right direction at least. But, since the news had
been announced, nothing had happened.

I wanted to sound the alarm, but I couldn't count on the media to
properly relay the message. I turned to the Major League Baseball
authorities and asked them to make the public aware of what everyone in the organization already knew: the relaunch plan was at a
dead end. Ménard and his group had run out of gas. And baseball's
most recent market studies showed baseball was in freefall in
Montreal: 67% of respondents said they were completely uninter-
ested in the future of the Expos.

In New York, there was hesitation about stirring up public
opinion on this subject. The executives preferred to adopt a
wait-and-see attitude. But on June 28, legal counsel Bob DuPuy
imposed a new deadline on Ménard, one he failed to meet. Then
came another one; Ménard ignored that one as well. Knowing it
wasn't highly regarded in Montreal, Major League Baseball didn't
seem to want to make matters worse by denouncing the consortium's irresponsibility.

The poor results obtained by the continuing partners left them vulnerable to the demands of prospective investors. Desperate, wanting to complete the financing structure and the new stadium at any cost, the consortium was in a position of weakness.

In 1991, art dealer Jeffrey Loria had shown interest in becoming a member of the consortium and investing a significant amount— on the condition, obviously, of taking over control of the team. The proposal had been rejected. He then tried to buy the American League Baltimore Orioles for $170 million but was outbid by current owner Peter Angelos.

A few years later, I approached Loria and other investors to purchase the City of Montreal's shares in the Expos, without success. Loria then had to wait until another team became available.

In 1998, Jacques Ménard, Mark Routtenberg, and Sam Eltes once again contacted the American multimillionaire and asked him to become the lead investor in the Montreal Expos. The proposal appealed to Loria. Impressed by what the team had accomplished with such meagre resources, he'd always praised the organization. Owning the team would be the realization of a dream he'd cherished since he was a child in New York, where he grew up idolizing the Yankees.

CHAPTER 21

Loria's Demands

During the summer of 1999, it appeared obvious to all observers that Jeffrey Loria was the only investor capable of saving the team. The New York art dealer met numerous times with the relaunch committee in the hope of coming to an agreement on apportioning powers within the new consortium. There was no doubt, considering his financial input, that Loria would become the new general partner. But his arrival hardly made everyone jump for joy.

Stephen Bronfman had also confirmed his interest in participating in the relaunch of the team, but he was conscious of the risk involved in the arrival of Loria as the general partner. On several occasions, Bronfman and his financial advisor, Mark Smith, met with Bud Selig and Major League Baseball president Paul Beeston. Beeston was convinced Bronfman could increase his stake if necessary. He even foresaw him investing $100 million. Beeston believed Bronfman could replace Loria if the American couldn't come to terms with the continuing partners. That was plan B. He was wrong. Bronfman had no intention of becoming the majority shareholder in the team.

No matter. The involvement of Stephen Bronfman in Jacques Ménard's group reassured Major League Baseball. To that point, Selig had been convinced the current partners couldn't guarantee the team's survival. The high-profile arrival of Bronfman gave the partners and the relaunch committee credibility once again. Selig was a good friend of Stephen's father, Charles Bronfman. The two men had a lot of respect for one another. As well, Beeston had confidence in Smith, Stephen Bronfman's financial counsel.

During this time, negotiations with Loria dragged on. He'd already confirmed his financial intentions. In February, he committed to invest $75 million on the condition his Quebec partners also put in $75 million. Well aware of not being their first choice (they would have preferred Stephen Bronfman), but also aware they had no alternative investor and were therefore vulnerable, Loria took advantage of the situation to exact a host of concessions. He threatened to walk away if the partners resisted. The two parties constantly put off important decisions, notably about control of the team. They could agree only on the details. The negotiations must have broken down at least 20 times. The relaunch committee didn't give up, obviously. They didn't have a choice. After announcing to the media on several occasions that the deal was nearly done, that the champagne was already on ice, the partners realized the negotiations were at a dead end. Yet they kept trying.

The presence of David Samson, Loria's stepson, at these negotiating sessions annoyed the continuing partners. They found him arrogant and rude and didn't appreciate his know-it-all attitude. To get him out of the way, the partners suggested to Loria that Samson be entrusted with supervision of the new stadium project. Loria refused. He'd promised another job to his stepson, a more prestigious job—that of chief operating officer. Everyone was sure that job would be filled by Roger Samson, Ménard's right arm, who'd been with the Montreal Manic soccer club. No way, said Loria. It would be David Samson, or there would be no deal.

Loria wasn't opposed to naming a francophone to the job, but he didn't want to entrust it to someone chosen by the current partners. He didn't want to find himself with a "spy" sent in by Ménard and the others.

There was more. One day I received a copy of the letter of

intent between Loria and the consortium, according to which the Expos agreed to pay Loria $1 million U.S. to compensate him for the expenses he'd incurred up to that point in his attempt to acquire the team. It was an agreement Ménard and the other members of the relaunch committee had negotiated.

For his part, the commissioner fervently hoped I'd stay on until the process came to its conclusion. Observers in Montreal and elsewhere knew the situation would be short-lived, but Major League Baseball felt cornered by Ménard and his group. The commissioner refused to consider allowing the team to move. I was at the end of my rope.

In my view, they were skating around crucial issues, and no solution was in sight for the short term. Another year might go by without any progress, and the franchise, already fragile, was headed toward certain death. I therefore asked the commissioner to put an end to my ordeal. I'd always been loyal to him over the years, and we were friends. He regretfully promised to do everything he could to speed up my departure.

I'd accepted the $15 million buyout for my shares many months before. Given I'd invested $5 million in the early years, the return on my investment exceeded 12%, and that was acceptable to me. The process supposed to lead to the repurchasing of my shares in the club was set in motion; four long months would go by before it reached its conclusion. One of the clauses accepted by the partners and ratified by Major League Baseball imposed a penalty if the team left Montreal within the next five years. The penalty started at $5 million and decreased by $1 million every year. I was pushing the envelope.

Negotiations between Loria and his prospective partners continued with the requisite highs and lows, which were equally frustrating for both sides. During the fall, the members of the consortium constantly went back on their decisions, all the while trying to find a mechanism that would allow them to control Loria. They didn't want to find themselves with another . . . me. For that reason, they asked the new owner to accept the creation of an executive committee, made up of Jacques Ménard, Pierre Michaud, Stephen Bronfman, David Samson, and Loria himself.

In theory, this committee would approve any changes to the team's leadership, notably the "control party" required by the terms of Major League Baseball but also the chief executive officer, the chief operating officer, and the chief financial officer. The committee would also have input on the team's payroll, construction estimates for the new stadium, and the team's annual budget if expenses increased more than 10% per year or more than 25% over five years.

Loria accepted the idea of this committee, which reassured the members of the consortium. In my opinion, Loria committed to this process with a lot of good faith. It was only later, when the relationship with his partners deteriorated, that he was very tough on them.

Loria informed his partners he intended to double the team's payroll, from $15 million to $30 million. The goal, he explained, was to improve the club by making it more competitive and, consequently, enticing more fans to Olympic Stadium. His goal was to reach 80% of Major League Baseball's average payroll within three or four years. The partners were thrilled with the proposal.

The relaunch committee and Loria had agreed Ménard and his partners would take care of finding the financing for construction of the new stadium and would look at obtaining an increase in revenues from local television rights since they knew the people involved well. They'd also try to increase advertising revenue. And that wasn't all. The partners agreed that Loria and Samson, as the team's managing general partner and chief operating officer, would receive salaries totalling approximately $10 million over the next three years.

At the beginning of October, the two sides finally came to an agreement—there wasn't much more the consortium could give up! With this agreement, Loria confirmed his intention to invest $75 million, but he'd only hand over the entire amount on the day Ménard and his group completed their share of the financing. For the moment, Loria's investment would be $18 million. Stephen Bronfman, Jean Coutu, and Loblaws supplied an additional $3 million—$1 million each—for a total of $21 million. (They also committed later to investing an additional $9 million each in the new consortium, bringing their total investment to $10 million apiece.)

Part of this amount ($15 million) was earmarked for the repurchase of my shares; the remaining $6 million was used to buy back the shares of Aramark, also leaving the partnership because of Major League Baseball regulations preventing a company from owning shares in two teams (Aramark, which had taken over Versa Foods, had a small stake in the Boston Red Sox).

In short order, the new partners were supposed to finalize a second agreement in which Loria would increase his investment from $18 million to $75 million, while Ménard would bring in another $72 million to add to the $3 million from Bronfman, Coutu, and Loblaws. Loria was confident he could come up with the rest of his share. But could Ménard? In private, the partners would admit that they'd given up control of the organization for peanuts but that they'd had no choice.

Several weeks later, the 29 other Major League Baseball owners would unanimously accept the relaunch plan. And I'd give way to Loria, the new managing general partner. Bernard Landry would repeat we were behaving like colonials; where we once had a Quebec company run by Quebecers, we now had a company controlled by an American.

CHAPTER 22

The Press Conference

Yet another mega press conference, this time to announce the signing of the agreement between Jeffrey Loria and his partners, unfolded amid mass euphoria. There were plenty of congratulatory handshakes, slaps on the back, platitudes, and incidental clichés.

Jacques Ménard had saved the Expos! "At least the team's future is secure," Jack Todd wrote in the Montreal *Gazette*. "Major League Baseball believes in the solidity of this new partnership."

"At the start, we had no precise plan, no plan for a new stadium, no money, nothing at all," Ménard boasted. "We were just a group of friends of baseball who wanted to keep the team in Montreal. Nobody inside the organization wanted to assist us." And he added, proud of himself, "We had to save the team against its will." Ménard was on a roll. He stated 85% to 90% of the $150 million he needed to find was already in place or shortly would be; the identities of the investors would be unveiled in the coming weeks.

Mark Routtenberg added, "It took us more time than expected, but my partners and I did our homework."

Jocelyn Proteau, the team's "banker," said with assurance, "The recapitalization of the team will be completed by January 2001."

And the content of the deal with Loria? The members of the consortium were determined never again to "be powerless as they had been under Brochu." Ménard told Bertrand Raymond of the *Journal de Montréal*, "Loria has a reputation of being a tough businessman, but he's no tougher than I am. This time, I think he has met his match."

Loria had undoubtedly made a good impression. He'd come to Montreal on a few occasions, met the Expos' employees, played ball with his stepson on the future site of Labatt Park. As well, he could express himself in French. He said he adored Montreal. And, most of all, he loudly proclaimed what everyone wanted to hear: "We will do everything in our power to help the long-term survival of baseball in Montreal."

Loria was keen on the idea of a new downtown stadium. But after analysing the plans with his architects, he quickly realized the project as proposed was unworkable. Serious structural defects and inadequate materials selected because of the new budgetary restrictions compromised construction of the ballpark. So Loria decided to design the stadium he wanted, which would have a capacity of 40,000, not 35,000. That stipulation obviously led to major modifications to the construction estimates.

Loria quickly figured out he was dealing with partners who were evasive, untrustworthy, and used all sorts of tricks, a lot of smoke and mirrors. Protecting their images was what concerned them above all else, according to the new general partner. So it was understandable the relationship between the two sides soon deteriorated. The members of the consortium thought they could control Loria, for example, by creating an executive committee and requiring him to get their approval for the nomination of the CEO. He neatly navigated around this problem by not naming a CEO. As early as the executive committee's first meeting, when one of the partners made a remark about the way the club was being run, Loria turned to him and said, "You're not running the club; I am." After that, Loria sent financial advisor Joel Mael to represent him at committee meetings. For him, the committee existed only as a consultative body; it had no real authority.

Just prior to my departure at the beginning of December, I warned the new owner about the unusual group he'd be dealing with in the years to come. "Beware and, most of all, never trust them blindly," I told him.

Loria smiled. "I know. I've already realized it," he said. "The

214

more I see them go, the more I am convinced that you weren't the enemy. They were."

He was confident he could restore baseball's reputation in Montreal and succeed where others had failed. He was certain he could revive the public's interest in the Expos despite the numerous problems plaguing the team. Unfortunately, Loria grasped neither the size nor the scope of the difficulties the organization had gone through. He chose to get involved even though Major League Baseball had warned him about the problems.

Ménard and his associates now had to confirm the participation of the other investors—a mere formality, according to his comments on signing the agreement with Loria. But now it was his turn to discover he couldn't take Ménard's words as gospel.

Other than Stephen Bronfman, Jean Coutu, and Loblaws, who were already in for $10 million apiece, the new investors were slow to come forward. André Desmarais of Power Corporation showed interest, but he was just about the only one. Major League Baseball began to realize those prospective and allegedly serious investors—their names had been submitted to Major League Baseball for verification and investigation by the relaunch committee—were saying they'd declined to invest some time ago and didn't understand why they were on a list of confirmed investors. It appeared Ménard and his group would be unable to raise the $72 million still required.

Of the three committees formed at the October 7 meeting, the ones responsible for refinancing and stadium construction had come up with next to nothing. The sales of seat licences and corporate boxes were going nowhere, and the partners were unable to secure the sponsorship and advertising revenues they'd promised to bring in. The money from television and radio rights also wasn't there. The amounts offered were ridiculously small. Loria described the situation on that front as the equivalent of being 80th in the major leagues in revenue, so far were the numbers behind the next-worst team, ranked 29th out of the 30 teams.

There was still the Quebec government, which had committed to paying the interest on the $100 million loan the Expos would

need to build the downtown stadium. There was only one problem: no bank would lend the team the money even though the
stadium itself would be collateral. The banks wanted the franchise
itself to be pledged instead. The members of the consortium
would probably have accepted this strict condition. But Jeffrey
Loria and Bud Selig would have none of it.

CHAPTER 23

The Quagmire

The opening of training camp is usually an enjoyable time for everyone. It's the start of a new season; the players renew acquaintances, as do the fans, the sponsors, the marketing people. . . . But in March 2000 in Jupiter, the first training camp of the Jeffrey Loria era was a painful experience for the partners on several levels.

The two groups couldn't even agree on the most innocuous things—who'd be invited to the receptions, for example. Loria preferred to stay with his own people during those activities, and that frustrated the partners. They felt ignored and rejected. They also began to realize they didn't count much in the eyes of the new general partner.

Still in Jupiter, in a meeting during which, as usual, Loria rarely spoke (David Samson or Joel Mael usually spoke for him), the subject of the new stadium was broached. The partners, dumbfounded, learned the revised costs for the new stadium would reach $250 to $300 million to ensure it conformed to the necessary standards. The partners would therefore have to absorb these increased costs. Loria then asked for a show of hands from those who were prepared to take on the responsibility. One hand went up—his own.

There was more. When he'd taken over the ball club, Loria had warned his partners he intended to increase the payroll over the next few years. The relaunch committee had applauded the decision but hadn't grasped all of its implications. On the one hand, if new investors joined the group, money wouldn't be lacking, and increasing the payroll wouldn't be a problem. On the other hand, if there was no new money, the increased payroll would create a bigger debt—one the partners would have to absorb. The partners imagined the team would be run like the Cleveland Indians, where the increase in payroll coincided with the increase in revenues generated by the new stadium. But in Montreal, in the absence of a new stadium, the partners would have to foot the bill themselves. In addition, they'd have to absorb the more than $200 million of debt the team would accumulate over the next four years or so.

The numbers put forth by Loria and his team surprised the partners. They were dealing with a situation they could neither understand nor accept. They hadn't expected the situation to deteriorate so rapidly. They expected a small loss that could be underwritten by increased investment from some of the partners, a process that would dilute the shares of those who elected not to follow suit. Cut payroll. Trade the players making too much money. Keep it bare bones, they said to Loria. We have to live within our means.

The new managing general partner refused. "Those who want to help me absorb the loss, raise your hands," he asked. It was the now-infamous cash call, the one everyone dreaded.

No response.

As he expected, Loria was the only one willing to contribute.

He refused to cut payroll. He also refused to take on the responsibility of financing the new stadium until the members of the consortium confirmed the injection of new capital. Having realized by now how "unproductive" his partners were, Loria obviously didn't want to risk assuming a huge debt—which threatened to become permanent—all by himself.

Instead of investing more, as Loria had requested, the partners decided to lend him the money he needed. When a second cash call was made a few months later, they refused to get involved. Loria would have to cover their share of the expenses.

In an emotional voice, Raymond Bachand of the Solidarity Fund asked Loria to step down. Give us the keys back, Bachand basically said to him, and we will return your $18 million and take back control of the organization. It was too late. Loria had no intention of selling his shares. Not then. Not ever. But you have to wonder what the cash-strapped partners would have done had Loria accepted their offer.

What happened next was predictable. Loria alone covered the cash call, therefore increasing his percentage of ownership in the team. The others quickly became minority partners. Today, in 2002, their investment represents less than seven percent of the total current value of the team. Their equity in the team rapidly shrank from 72% to less than seven percent; Loria now owns nearly 93%.

The consortium's biggest mistake, according to their own analysis, was failing to simultaneously close the two deals they'd negotiated with Loria. With the first agreement, he took control of the club, the three new partners put in $1 million each, and I was out. With the second agreement, to be signed quickly, Loria would add $57 million, and his co-owners would put in their remaining $72 million. When Loria realized his partners could barely manage the $30 million from Bronfman, Coutu, and Loblaws, he decided to stand pat. The partners were so certain they'd be able to come up with the money they immediately ceded control to Loria. They thought they were much more high performance than they really were.

For the media, it was the same old story. Now that I was gone, Loria became public enemy number one. The partners alerted the journalists and began a smear campaign aimed at both Loria and Samson.

The public turned against the two men, especially Samson, who fulfilled the same operational duties I had. Even if he was considered by his stepfather to be not only an excellent manager but also a fantastic human being, Samson didn't project a positive image among Montrealers. The young executive vice president regularly kept visitors waiting. He was often late for important meetings. Many found him rude, crude, and inattentive. Samson came across to everyone as pretentious and arrogant.

One of his first decisions when he came on board was to refuse to pay bills in full from the suppliers and advisors who'd worked on the relaunch of the club. Lawyer's bills, for example, but also bills from advertisers, financial advisors, communications firms. . . . Samson started to dither, saying he only wanted to pay half. He turned off a lot of people with that behaviour. Irritated by Samson, several companies associated with the ball club decided to end that association.

Once more Montreal became the laughingstock, and the embarrassment, of Major League Baseball. The partners began blaming everyone but themselves for the failure of the initiative. After casting blame on Loria and Samson, they criticized Major League Baseball for failing to do its homework on the new general partner. Yet those partners had approached the art dealer to speed things up! To this day, the members of the consortium still don't know who Loria's associates are.

Loria, for his part, blamed his partners for sabotaging his efforts to relaunch professional baseball in Montreal. But he couldn't count on the support of Major League Baseball's executives. Bud Selig and his colleagues found the Loria-Samson duo argumentative and arrogant. As well, the commissioner didn't appreciate the manner in which Loria treated Stephen Bronfman throughout this process.

Ménard's group was also targeted. Major League Baseball found their behaviour to be deplorable. And the lack of respect displayed by the relaunch committee toward the Office of the Commissioner wasn't forgotten.

We have to expect some kind of settling of accounts eventually. In this conflict, only Stephen Bronfman will walk away with his head held high.

Seeing the dangerous waters into which the Montreal franchise, yet again, had plunged, and having no confidence in Ménard and his group, Selig allowed Bronfman to try to put together a new group of Canadian investors with the goal of taking back control of the team. Major League Baseball wanted to help him push Loria aside. Not only did Bronfman want to keep the Expos in Montreal, but he also wanted to buy the Montreal Canadiens. To that end, he foresaw the creation of a megacompany that would include the two professional sports clubs. He said he was prepared to invest $50 million of his own money. But Bronfman found no takers. He was forced to abandon his initiative.

Major League Baseball was ready to help the partners as long as they helped themselves by following Loria's example and investing in the team. It was prepared to repurchase the partners' shares at full value, even after dilution. Later it changed its position.

In short order, Loria went from hero to villain. The "dastardly plot" that first appeared during the Brochu era resurfaced again. The Expos' new general partner obviously had only one thing in mind: moving the team somewhere in the United States, with the complicity of Major League Baseball. The members of the consortium accused Loria of poor management, of failing to run the organization responsibly; he denied the accusations. Once more the partners used the media to divert attention from their latest failure. It was all Loria's fault; they themselves had done nothing wrong. As Bronfman put it so well in referring to the new consortium, "We all look like asses!"

Today the Expos are bogged down in a quagmire from which they cannot extricate themselves. The team continues to depend heavily on the assistance of others, thanks to the revenue-sharing program. The increase in payroll advocated by the new general partner obviously didn't bring about the desired results. The club is worse than it was before, and the fans have continued to abandon Olympic Stadium.

In August 2001, in an article in *La Presse*, Alexandre Pratt reported that after 61 games the average attendance at home games was 8,655 fans. "It is by far the worst attendance in Major League Baseball. There are triple-A teams with better results," he wrote. Pratt added the 2001 season was one of the worst in terms of attendance in the history of the Expos. In fact, it was the worst ever. The average attendance of 7,648 per game was even lower than that in 1976, the team's final season in Jarry Park before the move to Olympic Stadium.

The media were paying less and less attention to the team. Pratt noted in his article that both *La Presse* and the *Journal de Montréal* left the coverage of the August 11 game against the Milwaukee Brewers to La Presse canadienne, the French-language wire service. It was the first time in 33 years the two major French-language dailies in the city didn't send their own reporters to cover an Expos game played in Montreal. *La Presse* had only sporadically travelled with the team in recent years. The *Journal de Montréal* virtually stopped following the Expos at the 2001 all-star break. The *Gazette* stopped going on the road in mid-August, with the exception of the final weekend of the season in New York.

Professional baseball can no longer survive in Montreal. The harm has been done; the situation is beyond redemption. With their skulduggery, false accusations, and smear campaigns, added to their complete lack of understanding of the game, the members of the consortium needed only a few years to destroy one of the most remarkable and productive organizations in Major League Baseball.

What will the commissioner do now with the hot potato the Expos have become? There are two solutions available to Major League Baseball: move the club or disband it.

I was surprised to hear that the contraction of several teams was seen as a solution, albeit only a partial one, to the industry's economic problems. Contraction is a bad idea. The optics aren't good; it's a bad omen, a breach of trust. And it does nothing to reassure the fans, the advertisers, the sponsors, the reporters, and all those involved in the game to see Major League Baseball amputate a couple of its limbs. If this were to happen, it would be a clear indication of a profound malaise in the industry. Individuals and corporations will think twice before associating their names with it, especially after the fairly recent births of two new teams in Arizona and Tampa Bay. The contraction of one or several teams would be an admission of an inability to properly manage the business. The consequences would be tragic not only in the cities that would lose their teams but also at the minor-league level since four, five, and sometimes six cities would then lose their affiliation with the big club.

It's no surprise politicians at the federal, state, county, and municipal levels became involved in the case of the Minnesota Twins, the team targeted for contraction along with the Expos. When this happens, the judiciary necessarily follows; investigations are initiated, and the national spotlight is shone on an unpleasant situation.

The logical question to be asked is this: why contract when there are cities—Washington, DC, being number one on the list—looking for teams? Surely there are other cities capable of supporting a Major League Baseball team in the foreseeable future. The threat of contraction creates uncertainty and negativity that will drag on throughout the upcoming season and perhaps longer. If the Twins are sold to a new owner, the possibility of building a new stadium is revisited, and the contraction threat fades in Minnesota, which other team will then be abolished? Will the political and legal circus we've witnessed over the winter start anew in another city?

After witnessing the wholesale relocation of ownership and key personnel from Montreal to south Florida, Major League Baseball may now be faced with an even worse situation: a team in Montreal for its final season with attendance at worse-than-embarrassing levels. More uncertainty, more speculation, and more evidence that something is terribly wrong. Surely relocating the Expos would have been a better solution. The contraction issue may just give baseball, already teetering on the edge, one final push into the abyss. Contraction will also aggravate the relationship between the owners and the Players Association and could compromise negotiations concerning renewal of the collective bargaining agreement.

In my estimation, contraction of two teams—or four, for that matter—isn't a solution to Major League Baseball's problems. Many teams with competent personnel at every level that survived the cuts will still never take part in the postseason, simply because they can't hold their own financially with wealthier clubs. This is baseball's biggest problem, and it has to be solved right now. The fans know it. People who follow the game have noted it. The owners are aware of it. The gap between baseball's rich and poor teams has to be significantly narrowed as quickly as possible.

In July 2000, the Blue Ribbon Panel on Baseball Economics handed in its report. Clearly, sensibly, and eloquently spelled out were the facts that the money available as part of the revenue-sharing program had to be increased and that teams suffering from insurmountable problems had to be relocated. If those recommendations were put into action, there'd be no need for contraction.

Some owners will oppose those measures, of course. Their arguments will always be the same: that their revenues are the result of local investment and must remain where they are earned and that those revenues are reflected in the price they paid for their particular franchise. They're prepared to share revenues to a certain point—but not to the point required to set the game right. If a team can't survive in a given market, they say, move it to a better location.

For a long time, I maintained Major League Baseball's problems were the result of contentious labour relations between the owners and the Players Association. This is fundamentally an ownership problem even though the players' union doesn't appear to want to participate in reformulating the existing economic system. Now I'm more and more convinced Commissioner Selig's legacy will depend more on his ability to create a healthy competitive balance between the teams than on resolving labour questions. Reducing the economic disparity between the teams operating in small, "weak" markets and those that are well off is the only solution to the industry's problems, and the system will adjust to it.

If the wealthier owners can't see the obvious advantages that would benefit the game as a whole, they'll have to be pushed aside. The commissioner and those who run the other teams will have to find a way to institute the necessary changes. That is the challenge that lies ahead for Bud Selig. I sincerely believe that with his leadership, if he pursues this goal aggressively, he will succeed.

Conclusion

I am very concerned about the future of professional sports in Canada. With the exception of Toronto, all Canadian cities boasting professional sports teams risk losing them one day. Many teams are already hanging by threads.

Toronto has a clear advantage over the other large cities in the country, notably because of its location. The nerve centre of the country, it's where all the important business and industrial decisions are made. As well, southern Ontario's large population allows it to sustain professional teams in several sports. And the television rights fees, larger than in the rest of the country, guarantee hockey, baseball, and basketball teams much higher revenues than anywhere else in Canada.

Yet the situation is beginning to deteriorate there as well. The Blue Jays, previously considered a solid value by Major League Baseball and even the envy of some large-market, U.S.-based teams, are now losing significant dollars. Today the Blue Jays take advantage of the revenue-sharing program just as the Expos do.

The direct consequence of always finding oneself on a respirator is a lack of competitiveness. On occasion, a year can be filled with hope, and a team can be competitive. But as soon as the postseason arrives, that hope disappears. The most prosperous teams, those with substantial payrolls, are usually the teams that win. They can sign elite players, often free agents looking for bigger paycheques. In Canada, neither the Blue Jays nor the Expos—especially the

Expos—can compete with the American clubs at that level; the revenues simply aren't sufficient.

Several elements contribute to the Canadian teams' difficult situation. Obviously, the weakness of the Canadian dollar seriously handicaps teams in this country. In addition, a Canadian's ability to spend money on entertainment is far less than that of his or her American counterpart. These two issues aren't limited to the world of professional sports; they are facts of Canadian life that can't be ignored.

Governments' attitudes toward the problems faced by professional sports teams is one of noncollaboration. Governments prefer to play the salary-inflation scandal card, fed by negative public reaction. We always get the same old song and dance from them: we cannot come to the aid of incredibly wealthy owners and grossly overpaid players, they claim, while hospitals are closing down beds. Fix your industry, and we'll consider looking at it. It's a simplistic policy that is harmful in the long term. Instead of depreciating professional sport, they should try to better understand how it contributes to the economic, social, and cultural vitality of Canadian cities.

In fact, governments are the ones who benefit the most from the existence of professional sports teams because of the income taxes on players' salaries, the taxes paid by team employees, the sales taxes, and the municipal taxes. When a club moves to the United States, those revenues go with it. In Canada, too many levels of government prefer to stand back and watch the teams leave instead of taking on a leadership role in the resolution of this endemic problem.

But governments aren't the only ones to blame. The professional teams also bear their share of responsibility in this mess. Cut off from the rest of the real world, refusing to admit the indecency of spiralling salaries and spoiled athletes who too often threaten to withhold their services, the professional sports business is now out of control. In this context, it's difficult to convince governments and citizens of the usefulness of sports teams and their contributions to the country's economy.

Another aspect complicates the situation even further. For the past few years, Montreal has preferred to encourage short-term sporting events rather than athletic competitions spread out over an entire season. A few days of Formula One racing or a week of tennis or golf are full of charm and require no long-term commitment. While those events are useful and meet a need, they can't take up all the room. In 10 or 20 years, will we still be content with these sporadic competitions? Once the Expos have disappeared from the local landscape after more than 30 years, how will the hole left by their departure be filled? In 30 years, when the Expos will have long been eliminated or transferred to the United States, Montreal will find itself much like Washington is today, a great city, certainly, but one lacking a Major League Baseball team. And the sporting public won't be happy about it.

But the big question remains: could the Expos have survived in Montreal? Many observers for whom I have the greatest respect consider, quite rightly, that there are too many negative factors conspiring against the team's survival in Montreal—economic, political, social, and cultural factors. I prefer to ask the question another way. Could we have created an environment favourable to success? I think we could have, but it would have required major efforts from all concerned.

After giving it considerable thought, and after numerous consultations, I proposed a well-thought-out plan for a new ballpark in downtown Montreal. This ballpark would certainly have contributed to that hoped-for environment. But for this facility to become reality, we first had to ensure construction was financed jointly by the business community and the three levels of government. The club couldn't find itself under an unbearable mountain of debt, nor could it assume the exorbitant costs of maintenance or an onerous municipal-tax burden. All the revenues generated by the team had to remain within the organization. Once again it's imperative to remember that the governments quickly recoup their investments via income taxes and various other taxes and that their commitments can be totally justified.

The new stadium would have met strict engineering and architectural criteria to attract the greatest number of fans on a continuing basis. Compromising construction quality would have had dramatic and irreversible effects. Those who aren't aware of what has been going on in recent years, in cities where new stadiums have been built, might consider our requirements excessive. They weren't. On every level, they respected the standards established by recognized experts in the field and were accepted everywhere in the United States.

Our other economic problems, notably those related to the weakness of the Canadian dollar, would have been dealt with and resolved one at a time, at the appropriate time. We would have found ourselves in the same situation as a dozen other clubs that have renewed their facilities. We would have continued to battle for changes to the industry's economic structure so the redistribution of revenues would benefit teams operating in smaller markets.

The market studies we produced confirmed our plan. With a new stadium, the public—particularly the anglophone public—would have made up with their team. The sparse crowds at Olympic Stadium would have been replaced by large and enthusiastic crowds at the new ballpark, as was the case when the Alouettes moved to Percival Molson Stadium. For the first time in its history, the ball club would have had a genuine baseball stadium. The Expos wouldn't be the first team slated for contraction.

The comments from the media would have become more favourable since the climate would have been one of renewal and rebuilding. And with an improved team, the public would have displayed newfound pride. The depressing memories of the years when we had to get rid of our star players would have faded eventually; in their place would have been a promising future and the realistic hope of a trip to the World Series.

What would the atmosphere inside the consortium have been like? Difficult to imagine. Even with a renewed team pointed toward the future, the frustrated and dissident partners would have continued to make themselves heard. Perhaps the team's improved situation would have encouraged replacements to come forward.

230

Perhaps a merger of the Canadiens and the Expos could have been considered when Molson put the club up for sale. We could have been thinking big instead of small.

Lastly, even if we came within a hair of succeeding in the negotiations with Vice Premier Bernard Landry, they ultimately ended in failure. We failed because Premier Lucien Bouchard lacked vision. He didn't grasp the importance of associating the government with an organization that wanted nothing more than the success of an initiative all citizens could be proud of.

Bouchard preferred to listen to the dissident and frustrated partners, who believed they could, with their arrogance and a wave of their hands, turn everything they touched into gold. Instead, they turned everything into dust. Their failure was pathetic. They contributed to the decline of an institution that will soon disappear from the Montreal landscape. And along the way, they not only lost their investments but also their reputations as businessmen.

I can only be saddenned and disappointed by the failure of a dream, a dream I shared with all Expos fans.

Appendix

Montreal, February 17, 1999

Mr. Jacques L. Ménard
Chairman of the Board
Montreal Expos

Dear Sir,

Further to one of our telephone conversations yesterday (February 16) which touched upon, among other matters, the letter from Major League Baseball dated February 4, I have made my superiors aware of the accusation you levied of my being "manipulated" in the context of my work as a journalist covering the Expos story. The accusation is serious and cannot remain unaddressed, especially as it undermines my reputation for integrity, something I hold dear. It also attacks the reputation of Radio-Canada, hence my obligation to inform my superiors.

Please know, Sir, that I stand by what I told you yesterday, that is to say that I have not been manipulated by anyone. Your silence over the last 10 days simply obliged me to turn to other sources of information in order to keep the public informed about the developments in the very hot story that is the survival of the Expos in Montreal.

The use of any information gathered during the course of our investigations is always pursuant to the editorial judgment of an entire team, whose criteria for making those judgments are beyond reproach.

Respectfully yours,

Daniel Poulin

[Translated by Stephanie Myles]

LABATT PARK
Seat License Sales Progression
of licenses and sales in millions of $

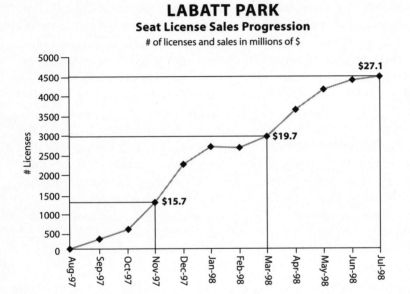

April 28, 1998

Mr. Jean Carle
Senior Vice-President, Corporate Affairs
Banque de developpement du Canada
5 Place Ville Marie, third floor
Montreal, Quebec
H3B 5E7

Re: Construction project by the Expos of a stadium in downtown Montreal

Dear Jean,

The following is a summary of the approaches made to the Government of Quebec by the Montreal Expos over approximately the last 15 months, as well as an outline of the anticipated results.

First, it is important to note that the conclusion reached by the Montreal Expos concerning the necessity of building a downtown stadium to ensure financial stability for the club, and solid prospects of progress on the baseball side, was arrived at only after careful consideration and draws upon comprehensive studies and analyses conducted over a period of more than a year.

We have examined in depth the numerous aspects and variables that are part of such a project, such as the Montreal market, the expected trends in the baseball industry over the next 10 years, the financial and economic impact, and social, urban and tourism factors, as well as the returns in terms of visibility and renown for Montreal. My partners and I have decided that, despite the many risks and the complexity of the project, we are inclined to put forth the energy and effort required to make it happen.

Armed with abundant documentation and solid data, we have embarked on a preliminary round of consultations that we would qualify as exploratory and informal with the Quebec government, dealing with privileged representatives such as the Minister of Finance, Mr. Bernard Landry, as well as Mr. Serge Ménard, former Minister responsible for the city of Montreal, and Mr. Robert Perrault, his successor and the current holder of this portfolio.

During this first stage, no form of financial assistance was solicited. However, we took pains to point out that we expected to return with specific proposals of financial assistance—which remains essential to the successful outcome of the project—but from the outset ruling out any possibility of direct subsidy.

Having been reasonably assured that the project was admissible and defensible from a business point of view as long as we respected the precondition of a mobilization of the greater Montreal business community, which would entail a financial contribution in the order of $100 million of the $250 million necessary for the project, we proceeded last June to a public announcement of the Expos' firm intention to build a new stadium, one that would allow Montreal to keep its professional baseball franchise.

As we understand it, the Quebec government's position concerning the project would be as follows:
- The precondition concerning the mobilization of the business world is fulfilled (more than 200 of the most influential people in the Montreal business community have agreed to get involved and to form subcommittees to lend a hand in the sale of seat licenses);
- Public opinion in Quebec is becoming increasingly favorable;
- Montreal's economic development is in urgent need of revitalization.

For all of those reasons, the Quebec government seems very willing to associate itself with the Expos in some fashion, whether it is a form of tax relief to be determined, such as dedicated taxes, or a partnership that would call upon a governmental agency such as the SGF, the Caisse, and even Loto-Quebec. We easily can devise a formula that would combine the two approaches and that we could qualify as "taxation-agency."

Given that the Quebec government went a long way in its aid proposals for the Quebec Nordiques, it surely would want to do as much and even more to ensure the Expos do not find themselves forced to leave Montreal and Quebec.

As far as the participation of the Government of Canada goes, we would hope to quickly reach agreement on the sale of the land in addition to obtaining assistance from the infrastructure program.

We would also hope that the federal government, the provincial government, and the Expos will agree without further delay to form an ad-hoc working committee whose principal objective would be to accelerate the decision-making process—which, we know, often is very slow to examine the various options proposed—to come to the Expos' aid and allow for a successful outcome of this magnificent project.

I have avoided bombarding you with numbers, but I thought it would be helpful to attach a summary that allows you to evaluate the scale of what is at stake in terms of the economic, urban and social impact as well as the benefits for Montreal in terms of visibility and image.

Without wanting to overstate the case, I consider that our downtown project will be the decisive factor in determining whether Montreal can turn the page on the problems it has suffered in recent years and move ahead, or continues to project the image of a city that will be in decline for the next 20 years.

Yours sincerely,

Claude R. Brochu
Montreal Baseball Club Inc.

CRB/mc

[Translated by Stephanie Myles]

IMPACT OF THE EXPOS' NEW DOWNTOWN BALLPARK

ECONOMY

DURING CONSTRUCTION (3 YEARS)
- Contribution to the Gross Domestic Product (GDP) of the province of $181 million.
- Creation of 3,785 jobs and payment of $117.8 million in salaries.
- Tax revenue of $37.3 million for the governments

AS FROM THE OPENING OF THE NEW BALLPARK IN 2001
- Annual GDP contribution of $180 million
- 2,146 jobs maintained
- Annual provincial tax revenue of $41.1 million
- Annual federal tax revenue of $36 million

Source: Ernst & Young LLP

TOURISM

- Annual number of tourists from outside Quebec attending Expos games*
Currently: 121,000   New ballpark: 200,000

For two out of every three, baseball is the principal reason for their visit to Montreal.

- Economic impact on an annual basis, resulting from the spending of tourists from outside Quebec who come to Montreal specifically for baseball**

	Currently (in $millions)	New ballpark (in $millions)
Total revenue (GDP)	22.6	35.9
Tax revenue	14.7	26.2
Employment	269	427

VISIBILITY

The value received by Montreal beginning in 2001 in terms of the media visibility across North America is valued at more than $21 million*** per year. This visibility comes notably from the mention of the city's name and/or the broadcasting of images:

- during the television broadcast of games by the visiting clubs in their respective markets;
- during the broadcast of these same games on the radio;
- during newscasts across America;
- in numerous newspaper articles

*Leger & Leger
** Ernst & Young LLP
*** Joyce julius and Associates.

Office of the Commissioner
MAJOR LEAGUE BASEBALL

September 30, 1998

L. Jacques Menard
Chairman, Partnership Committee
Montreal Expos
1501 McGill College Avenue
Suite 3200
Montreal, Quebec H3A3M8

Dear Mr. Menard:

I have reviewed the various press reports out of Montreal over the past several days involving
the activities and comments of you and others members of your partnership. I am very
distressed that as members of the Montreal Expos Partnership, you have improperly taken it
upon yourself to comment publicly on issues so critical to the survival of the franchise. As
you know, we have clear and longstanding ownership guidelines and rules that govern the
operation of our Clubs. I made reference to them as recently as my letter of yesterday to Mr.
Brochu, which I understand was forwarded to you.

The success of the Montreal franchise is critical to Baseball. I have personally requested a
visit with both the Prime Minister and the Provincial Premier to explore solutions involving
your franchise. Your public comments – contrary to our guidelines – could be very disruptive
to the efforts we are making. Baseball operates by having a control person responsible for
each franchise. Claude Brochu is your franchise's control person. As you also know, he
serves on the Major League Executive Council, which acts as my paramount advisory board.
He also serves on the National League Executive Council and as Chairman of the Baseball
Operations Committee. Your franchise is well represented at the highest levels of Baseball.

I must request that your public comments and speculation cease, and that you work within the
framework of our ownership guidelines through Mr. Brochu. Thank you for your cooperation.
I assure you, I have only the interests of your franchise and Baseball in mind.

Very truly yours,

Allan H. Selig
Commissioner

cc: Claude Brochu

350 Park Avenue, New York, NY 10022 (212) 339-7800

CONFIDENTIAL

January 20, 1999

Destinataires/To: Fonds de Solidarité des travailleurs
                du Québec   Raymond Bachand
                Télémédia Inc.   Claude Beaudoin
                Coup de Circuit L.P.   Claude R. Brochu
                M & S Sports Inc.   Avie Bennett
                                          Paul Bennett
                Cascades Inc.   Alain Lemaire
                Bell Canada Enterprises Inc. Guy Marier
                Nesbitt Burns Inc.   L. Jacques Ménard
                Univa (Provigo) Inc.   Pierre Michaud
                Fédération des Caisses Populaires
                de Montréal et de l'Ouest de Montréal Jocelyn Proteau
                114114 Canada Inc.   Paul Delage Roberge
                Freemark Investments Inc.   Mark Routtenberg
                Canadian Pacific Limited   Norman Wale
                Versa Services Ltd   Fiduciaire/Trustee:
                                          Claude R. Brochu

Expéditeur/From: Laurier M. Carpentier

RE: REFLECTIONS ON THE FUTURE OF THE MONTREAL PROJECT

As we now are approaching a point in time when decisions having significant public relations and financial repercussions must be made, I would like to share with you my reflections on the project's and industry's principal trends. I also wish to discuss with you the nature of my continued involvement with the project and with the team.

Construction

As directed by the Limited Partners, a structured bid process was launched. While I believe that our efforts in this area were extremely well done in the circumstances, **I do not believe that the process currently being pursued is in the best interest of the Partnership**. We have eliminated a planning effort that is normally required to provide a proper level of definition as regards content, scope and overall quality standards. I point out that a baseball park is not a generic product and that recent experience in other cities has shown that the fan experience can be significantly improved through careful planning and precise adjustment of every element of the project. I believe that the lack of a proper level of definition of what the owner requires creates a significant risk that there will either be cost overruns, reductions in the scope and quality of the project to levels that will be functionally, operationally or esthetically unacceptable or quite simply a project that will not meet with fan acceptance.

CLUB DE BASEBALL MONTRÉAL INC., MONTREAL BASEBALL CLUB INC.   . . 2
C.P. 500, SUCCURSALE "M" / P.O. BOX 500, STATION "M", MONTRÉAL, QUÉBEC H1V 3P2 (514)253-3434 FAX: (514)253-8282

In construction and development there is no such thing as an iron-clad upset price contract and this is especially true on a special purpose tailor-made project such as a baseball park. **We are not building to shell here**. Responsibility for any owner induced after-the-fact modifications, any time delays in the delivery of owner comments and approvals and insistence on the overall quality standard that is required to assure performance and longevity will ultimately have to be negotiated. The environment that prevails in a fast track project is not conducive to settling such items as the work progresses and we can be assured that the contractor will insist upon some possibility of financial relief in the construction contract.

I believe that the current timetable that predicts an opening of the ballpark in mid-season 2001 is unrealistic.

The commencement of construction is contingent upon: the recapitalisation of the team; the donation of the land; the commitment of all ballpark funding; the exoneration of property taxes; a certain base level of seat license sales; an acceptable zoning/development plan with City officials; the negotiation of a lease, and the approval of major league baseball. These matters cannot be successfully dealt within a time-frame that will allow for commencement of construction during the summer months. The complexity of the challenge that you have undertaken is such that I believe that an opening date at the opening of the 2002 season represents a significant challenge.

The process could be shortened by commencing construction before the above have been definitively dealt with but such a decision would entail significant risk to the Partnership. Do not expect to obtain favorable treatment in any area after the decision to go ahead is made public.

We must also bear in mind that the arrival of a significant investor will necessarily create some delays in the process. A serious investor will certainly insist upon the opportunity to extensively review all plans and contractual arrangements with the possibility of making modifications.

I do not believe that the current process can be followed to its logical conclusion within risk parameters that I find acceptable.

Zoning

The zoning status of the site must be defined with City officials. These officials, sense that there is currently a vacuum at the ownership level. They also desire to be very responsive to different interest groups and have been gradually increasing the scope of their demands. I do not believe that the incorporation of a 45' band of residential type housing along the length of de la Montagne is desirable or feasible and will ultimately lead to a problem on the Peel Street side of the project.

I do not believe that an environment conducive to the negotiation of a feasible and well-contained zoning plan currently exists. It will not therefore be possible to negotiate an acceptable solution with the City until such time as it is clear that all the elements required for the project to happen are at hand and that there is clear direction from an identified ownership group. In any case, the acceptable risk parameters for the owners will have to be definitively set by someone in authority and insisted upon as a condition precedent to the project going ahead.

... 3

A lack of the proper level of resolve will only lead to increasing demands by City officials before and during the construction and we can anticipate that these demands will translate into timing delays and additional costs. If the go-ahead is committed to by the owner before a detailed development plan is agreed upon, the ultimate developer will lose all negotiating leverage with City planning officials.

This process, depending on the crystallization of the sponsorship element, could very well encompass an additional 6 to 12 months.

Marketing

The marketing program will have to be launched in order to garner funds and test market depth. **This must be done before construction commences.** I believe that any marketing offensive before having definitively eliminated the uncertainty as regards the ownership of the team, the financing of the ballpark and the long-term feasibility of baseball in Montreal, would be a serious mistake. The underlying uncertainty would ultimately lead to very modest results thereby further undermining the already fragile credibility of the project.

The seat license program has been reviewed. When you strip away all the cosmetic additions, the product currently proposed remains basically the one that was previously offered, i.e, the contractual right to occupy a specific seat during baseball games in the context of the purchase of the season ticket for the seat. The modifications that are proposed do not alter the essence of the product. Focus groups have indicated that there is a profound philosophical objection to this type of product.

In most other markets, the commencement of construction serves as the catalyst that is required to create a sense of scarcity and urgency and jump start license sales. I am not convinced that the Montreal market will exhibit the same tendency.

The creation of an alternate product; i.e., the offering of 2nd quality seats in the form of season ticket pre-commitments represents a much lower risk, lower cost method for potential clients to support the project. I believe that this product may ultimately meet with some success but there is a real risk that companies decide to exhibit their civic solidarity by committing to this lower risk product in lieu of the more demanding and costly seat license product. This product does not generate any funds for the construction program and is more easily canceled in the future.

I have to a great extent lost faith in the ability of the Montreal market to support baseball at the commitment and price levels currently required to sustain operations of a major league baseball team.

The feasibility of major league baseball in Montreal

In November, I felt the necessity of informing Mr. Brochu of my concerns regarding the evolution of the industry's cost structure and its potential impact on the Partnership's ability to field a competitive team in the context of a new ballpark. You were subsequently provided with my analysis by copy of a memo from Mr. Brochu to Mr. Ménard, dated November 2, 1998.

. . . 4

When attempting to assess the viability of a professional sports team at a given site, the following elements must be taken into consideration:

a) The direct relationship between a team's ability to generate discrete revenues and the team's potential on-field performance.

An initial study that we had commissioned with Ernst & Young, Chicago established that there is a direct, causal and circular relationship among the following: (stadium revenue-payroll-performance-attendance-stadium). The maintenance of sufficient levels of each of these links and the integrity of the linkage is essential for the survival of the franchise. If one of the links is deficient, a gradual but persistent downward spiral begins. The spiral eventually leads to the situation that the team currently faces of not being able to produce a team of sufficient quality to attract a sufficient fan base to pay for a quality team.

b) The standard accepted by the local fan base to determine a team's quality.

Viability is dependent upon consistently presenting a team that Montreal fans will consider to be of high quality.

I believe that in Montreal, the public's perception of a sports product's value is determined largely by a team's ability to participate in post-season play on a regular basis. Montreal's fixation with post-season play results from the region's historic affinity to professional hockey, a sport whose format is organized to eliminate only a few of the manifestly incompetent teams from post-season play. If all other factors are equal, the possibility of post-season play in the NHL is statistically probable while in baseball it is unlikely. This in the NHL leads to systematic inclusion in post-season play. I do not believe that the typical Montreal fan will adopt a frame of reference for baseball that will differ greatly from the hockey mindset.

A competitive but less than playoff quality team i.e., a team that consistently ranks as the 5th best team in its 15 team league will not garner nor will it maintain much goodwill in the Montreal market. A heavy dose of continuing goodwill is required to sustain the attendance levels as called for in the projections. Viability then becomes dependent upon providing for a team that has the potential to participate in post-season play on a regular basis.

The perception of quality with post-season play is best illustrated by recent fan reaction to the 1996 team that was only eliminated from post-season play during the last week of the season. The team was effectively a 5th place team but it is not remembered with any particular fondness by Montreal fans. I submit that such a team would have been greatly appreciated and the cause of much goodwill in most U.S. cities.

If post-season play is indeed the overriding determinant of fan perception in Montreal, the standard to which we will be held in the future is therefore much higher than it would be in other U.S. locations that are unencumbered by a dominant hockey tradition. We must be certain of our ability to meet the higher standard as established by our fans.

. . . 5

c) The adequacy of funds available for player payroll.

The future performance of the team and hence its potential to participate in post-season play on a regular basis depends on our ability to invest in player payroll. It is clear that player talent in the medium term becomes fully mobile and will concentrate in centers willing to pay the going rate. The cost of our player talent will therefore depend directly on the price levels established by the U.S. teams. The cost of player talent is in no way related to our potential local revenue levels.

Further analysis indicates that the cost of the more productive player talent i.e., the type of talent required to participate in post-season play, is largely established in a staggered trickle down manner with the cost of free agency talent representing the fountainhead of the process. With time, the better talent will become concentrated among those teams having the capacity to pay free agent market prices for a significant number of players leaving teams unable to commit at the same levels with a shortage of better talent and immature talent not yet having access to arbitration.

The extreme disparity in local revenues between the 7-8 most successful teams and the rest of the industry makes the use of average team salary as the benchmark to ascertain the adequacy of future investment in player payroll problematic. This is especially true in Montreal with its playoff or bust mindset. The top 7 teams in 1998 had average local revenues less revenue sharing of $102 million U.S. The average team's net local revenues were $65 million U.S. This indicates that the top 7 teams had the capacity to outspend the average by $37 million U.S each on a uniform number of roster positions.

We have set a benchmark of 90% of industry average payroll as our base level of feasibility. The team's financial prospects are now projected to allow for a player payroll equal to only an average of 87% of the industry average payroll over the initial 5 years. This performance is predicated upon an average attendance of 86% of capacity without climate protection in a Nordic climate with 50% of games usually scheduled in April, May and September. This represents a very aggressive projection and indicates extreme reliance on a high quality team year after year.

This projection indicates that the chances of participating in post-season play when measured as a function of the industry average payroll are not very encouraging.

The recent trends in the free agency market are what I consider to be most disquieting. While we seek to be able to join the average, it will in any case be increasingly difficult if not impossible for the average to compete against the top 7 – 8 teams as concerns play off participation. The results of the last 2 years when only 1 of 16 playoff eligible teams had a player payroll at or below the industry average confirms that in the future and because of huge disparities in purchasing power only those teams investing an amount in excess of the industry average will have access to post-season play.

An analysis of outstanding term player contracts which are generally indicative of better talent indicate that the average forward commitment of each of the top 8 revenue teams as of January 1999 is $120 million U.S. as compared to an average commitment of $81 million U.S. for each of the remaining 22 teams. In terms of future person/years under contract, the average of each of the top 8 revenue teams is 29 person/years as compared to an average of 12 person/years for each of the remaining 22 teams.

. . . 6

247

It is clear that free agent talent is concentrating at the higher end of the revenue spectrum.

On this basis, I believe that Major League Baseball even in the context of a new downtown ballpark is not viable in Montreal. The risk of embarking upon a spiral of decline and of creating a white elephant project is very real.

The industry is well aware of its revenue disparity and player payroll problems. To attempt to project future developments is always a hazardous undertaking but I will nevertheless venture forward. I believe that because of pressure from the significant number of teams now operating near or below the average and because of the evident talent disparity, a great number of teams will insist on a hard cap proviso at the expiration of the current labor agreement in 2001 or 2002. The union will adopt an intransigent stance that will cause a protracted work stoppage in either 2002 or 2003.

I believe that the duration of the stoppage could very well entail an entire season or more because of the now more generalized recognition of the gravity of the situation among the ownership group.

This type of occurrence would be especially damaging and costly to the Montreal franchise in the context of the opening of the new ballpark.

With time I believe that a settlement will be reached but I am not at all sure that the settlement will set the cost structure at levels which can accommodate all teams including a team operating with a structural requirement for an important annual infusion of revenue sharing, in a below average attendance market, in the lowest media market and in Canadian dollars.

My deliberations that the construction process that you have requested is risk laden, that the project cannot be safely delivered for the 2001 season and that in any case sufficient revenues are not available in Montreal to sustain a quality team have led me to conclude that I cannot in good conscience continue to participate in your efforts to build a new ballpark and to preserve major league baseball in Montreal. I therefore inform you that if you are successful at the efforts currently underway to recapitalise the team and to pursue the ballpark project, I will prevail myself of the benefits provided to me under the terms of my contract and I will cease my employment with the Expos.

I realize and accept fully that this conclusion on my part is highly dependent upon my subjective judgment as to the nature and timing of future events. I do not profess to having a lock-up on the ability to project future trends in Montreal and in baseball and I can easily and respectfully accept that you and others may not share my vision of things to come.

I will remain available to assist the Partnership to an orderly transition over the next few months.

. . . 7

I thank you for your support and encouragement during my tenure with the Expos. In the six (6) seasons that I have been with the team , I have always endeavored to aggressively serve the best interest of the entire Partnership. I have always attempted to provide you with high quality information and analyses in a timely manner and to allow you the benefit of any business judgment that I may have acquired over the years. I truly wish you luck with your project.

LMC/mc

Office of the Commissioner
MAJOR LEAGUE BASEBALL

February 4, 1999

<u>*VIA FACSIMILE - 561/775-9935*</u>

Mr. Claude Brochu
Montreal Expos
P.O. Box 500, Station M
Montreal, Quebec H1V 3P2

<u>*VIA FACSIMILE - 514/286-7287*</u>

Mr. L. Jacques Menard
c/o Nesbitt Burns
1501 McGill College Ave.
Suite 3200
Montreal, Quebec H3A 3M8

Dear Claude and Jacques:

On October 5, Commissioner Selig visited Montreal and met with each of you and with Premier Bouchard to explore the current situation with respect to the continued viability of the Montreal Expos franchise. There was general agreement among everyone that the only way that Major League Baseball could survive in your community was with a new stadium. It was also made clear that there would be no assurances that the current levels of revenue sharing would continue indefinitely. There was disagreement among you as to how best to achieve the goal of a new stadium. In order to allow the maximum opportunity for baseball to succeed in Montreal, a 150-day plan was devised, during which the limited partners were given an opportunity to raise the funds necessary to provide the basis for a new stadium and for continued operations going forward. During that period, Claude Brochu was to continue as your control person, as required by Baseball's rules, although Claude made it clear that he did not have confidence in the long-term viability of the limiteds' plan, and as a result, did not want to continue if the limiteds were successful in the short term in putting together their proposal. Consequently, it was necessary that you negotiate the price at which Claude would be willing to relinquish control <u>at such time</u> as all of the other conditions were met to build a new stadium and keep the Expos in Montreal. It was also established that an update would be given after ninety days to see what progress had been made toward the ultimate objective.

Over the past two weeks, Bill Bartholomay, Chairman of Baseball's Ownership Committee, Paul Beeston, President of Major League Baseball, Len Coleman, President of the National League, and counsel have been able to meet with each of you and discuss this matter further with Commissioner Selig. On the positive side, we are pleased that the limited partners have finalized a prospectus to go out to potential investors, although we understand that the group has now had some additional concerns about both the date the stadium can be put into operation, and some of the general economic assumptions. You have told us that you have determined to obtain another opinion from Ernst & Young about the feasibility of your economic plan. In addition, we were encouraged that the limiteds have located at least one potential investor in the club, Jeff Loria. Finally, we are pleased that you have apparently reached agreement on the price at which Claude will relinquish his ownership interest in the event the limiteds are able to satisfy the conditions precedent to keeping the team in Montreal. We are satisfied that Claude's continued participation as control person under these circumstances will have no negative impact on the limited partners' ability to raise money and implement their plan.

On the negative side, we are disappointed that there appears to be no progress with respect to government commitment, the zoning and municipal tax issues so critical to the development of the stadium have not gotten closer to resolution, the new investor base is not yet committed nor is it at this point particularly expansive, the revised stadium concepts have not yet been reviewed and we do not know if they will be acceptable or adequate to you or to Baseball, the anticipated shortfall on the revised seat license program has not been covered, and the limiteds now apparently may have the previously mentioned concerns about the economic assumptions in their prospectus.

It is imperative that Baseball and the Club move to a final resolution of this matter for all of the reasons discussed in October. Scheduling for the 2000 season, realignment issues and the finite window for the current revenue sharing arrangements, require that a determination be made whether the team can develop a realistic economic plan and successfully compete in Montreal even in a new venue.

In order to ensure that every effort possible has been made to allow that to happen, the Commissioner agrees to the following:

1.   Assuming we have all indemnities in place first, Jeff Loria shall be allowed access to the books and records of the Expos for purposes of doing his due diligence. It is expressly understood that Mr. Loria is considering his investment for the purpose of operating the team on a long-term basis in Montreal under all the conditions outlined in October, and that he will be provided a copy of this letter prior to commencing his diligence. Claude has emphasized, and it is critical that everyone be focused on the fact, that any change in control or sale of the club be

251

expressly for the purpose of keeping the team in Montreal and with an acceptable plan for doing so.

2. Subject to modifying the date of opening the stadium to 2002 and modifying the resultant economics, and subject to the limiteds' satisfaction with respect to the remainder of the representations contained in the prospectus, we agree to its release to those who have completed Baseball's required paperwork.

3. The limiteds will immediately provide to us a copy of the engagement letter with Ernst & Young and a copy of all draft reports prior to final issuance. We agree to provide such assistance to Ernst & Young as may be requested in the furtherance of their project.

4. The entry into a letter of agreement, subject to our approval, that Claude will relinquish his ownership interest for the amount you have negotiated, if, and only if, you are successful by March 6 in accomplishing the following:

   a. A feasible economic plan for the long-term operation of the team in Montreal, with adequate capital reserves, and with reasonable prospects for operating on a self-sufficient basis;

   b. A feasible plan for the construction of a new stadium consistent with the economic operation of the team.

It is understood that should the conditions of paragraphs 4 a. and b. not be fulfilled by March 6, or should the Ernst & Young study conclude that the continued operation of the Expos in Montreal is not feasible, Claude Brochu and Major League Baseball may take such actions as they deem appropriate in the best interests of the overall operation of Major League Baseball, including, without limitation, the sale and/or relocation of the franchise.

Sincerely,

Robert A. DuPuy
Executive Vice President of Administration
& Chief Legal Officer

cc: Commissioner Allan H. Selig
Paul Beeston
Leonard S. Coleman, Jr.
Thomas J. Ostertag
Robert J. Kheel

Office of the Commissioner
MAJOR LEAGUE BASEBALL

ROBERT A. DuPUY
Executive Vice President
Administration and Chief Leg

February 25, 1999

Via Facsimile- 514/286-7287

Mr. L. Jacques Menard
c/o Nesbitt Burns
1501 McGill College Ave.
Suite 3200
Montreal, Quebec H3A 3M8

Dear Jacques:

We have now had the opportunity to review your group's request for an indefinite extension of the March 6, 1999 deadline established by Commissioner Selig last October, along with the transcript and video of the press conference last Thursday, February 18. Your request has been discussed with Commissioner Selig, Bill Bartholomay, Paul Beeston, Len Coleman and counsel.

After careful consideration, and mindful of the efforts which have gone forward to date, we conclude that the March 6, 1999 deadline remains appropriate. To date, there has been no commitment for government support to keep the Expos in Montreal. On the contrary, Premier Brouchard has reiterated publicly his strong opposition to public financing for a new stadium and there was no mention of stadium financing in either the national or provincial budget. The plans for the construction of the stadium remain indefinite, and there appears to be no workable solution to the coverage of the shortfall in the event that the seat license program is not as successful as you have projected. Of course, if we are mistaken and some of these items are further along than I have suggested, or if progress is made by March 6, we would be certainly agreeable to discussing this with you further.

We, of course, will continue to work closely with you and your group through the next several weeks to try to move the process along as expeditiously as possible. We remain committed to doing everything possible to save baseball in Montreal, consistent with the overall interest of all thirty Clubs and the need to plan with respect to the 2000 season.

245 Park Avenue, New York, NY 10167 (212) 931-7800   http://www.majorleaguebaseball.com

Jacques, we appreciate the efforts that you and your group have made in attempting to put together a structure for going forward with baseball in Montreal. We also appreciate your acknowledgement at the press conference of the ultimate decision-making process, and your comment in response to a question posed by Mr. Tremblay reiterating that Claude Brochu is the control person and is in charge. I do, however, need to point out what we believe were certain factual inaccuracies at the press conference.

First, as you know, Jeffrey Loria was not approved by us to come in and replace Claude. In my letter of February 4, after recapitulating the status of this matter, we gave you permission to open your books to Mr. Loria and continue discussions with him to try to secure your financing. We have received no written understanding from Mr. Loria regarding either his financing or his commitment to keeping the team in Montreal. To leave the impression that we support the ouster of Claude in favor of a new control person is most unfortunate. Second, we did not suggest "certain modifications" to the prospectus that would delay the opening of the new stadium to 2002. Your own CFO concluded that 2002 was the only realistic date. We only asked that the prospectus be amended to reflect reality.

As I am sure you can appreciate, we were also very unhappy about the final three paragraphs of your prepared statement. The disparaging remarks made with respect to Claude were absolutely counter to all of our discussions and violated the integrity of the process. Finally, Mark Routtenberg's explicit recitation with regard to the offer to Claude and the financial analysis will only fuel further acrimony. As we have stated, we believe that the complaints about Claude were unjustified. Claude announced he would not go forward with a new group and he agreed to a buyout price if the team was kept in Montreal, which was one of the conditions precedent. No potential investor willing to keep the team in Montreal could possibly be deterred by that arrangement.

Thank you sincerely for your continued efforts on behalf of the franchise.

Very truly yours,

Robert A. DuPuy
Executive Vice President Administration
& Chief Legal Officer

cc: Commissioner Allan H. Selig
William Bartholomay
Paul Beeston
Claude Brochu
Leonard S. Coleman, Jr.
Thomas J. Ostertag
Robert J. Kheel

Office of the Commissioner
MAJOR LEAGUE BASEBALL

ROBERT A. DuPUY
Executive Vice President
Administration and Chief Legal Officer

March 17, 1999

Mr. L. Jacques Menard
c/o Nesbitt Burns
1501 McGill College Ave.
Suite 3200
Montreal, Quebec H3A 3M8

Dear Jacques:

On February 4, 1999, I wrote you and Claude outlining where we were with respect to the 150-day window for your group to raise the funds necessary to provide the basis for a new stadium and for continued operations going forward. We reiterated in that letter the conditions precedent to a successful resolution as set by Commissioner Selig in October and through our various discussions.

I also wrote you on February 25, in response to your request for an indefinite extension of the March 6 date and indicated that no extension would be forthcoming. We have had several conversations since that date about the status of your group's efforts, including your informal discussions with the national and provincial governments regarding their support and your continuing efforts to raise equity and conclude a transaction with Claude Brochu.

By your acknowledgment, none of these items has been finalized as of today's date. Each of the indications of support we have been provided is vague at most. In addition, as you are aware, the recent business plan submitted to our offices indicates more than two-thirds of your total revenue this year will come from central baseball sources. That alone highlights the gravity of the situation.

For some reason, there appears to be some confusion about the passage of March 6 and some tacit (or explicit) extension of that date. As Commissioner Selig made clear in his remarks last on March 6, there has been no extension granted and he is considering what should next occur in the best interests of all the Clubs, including the Expos. Until that time, the Partnership Agreement is operative and all communication between our offices and the Limited Partners should be directed through the General Partner. This is particularly critical given that all of our attentions need to be on the opening and conduct of the 1999 season, without further public distraction.

245 Park Avenue, New York, NY 10167 (212) 931-7800 http://www.majorleaguebaseball.com

Against that background, we believe a meeting among you, Paul Beeston and me, which may include Claude, would be appropriate to review all available options. We would be available anytime the week of March 29, beginning March 30. Your group formed a potential successor group last October 7, and your efforts were to coincide with the 150-day window provided by Baseball. Since that period has elapsed we are now governed by the existing partnership arrangement. We are, of course, willing to review any tangible and unconditional commitment which your group may have in fact obtained.

Thank you for your continued cooperation.

Very truly yours,

Robert A. DuPuy

cc: Commissioner Allan H. Selig
       Claude Brochu
       William Bartholomay
       Paul Beeston
       Leonard S. Coleman, Jr.
       Thomas J. Ostertag
       Robert J. Kheel

May 3, 1999

Mr. Raymond Bachand
Chief Executive Officer
Fonds de solidarité des travailleurs
et travailleuses du Québec
8717, rue Berri
Montréal, Québec
H2M 2T9

Dear Mr. Bachand:

We have read with much interest your comments of April 29th to the press regarding the " pitiful " state of the Club's marketing efforts. These comments are consistent with the tenor of some public messages that were expressed by members of the ownership group on prior occasions. Pitiful is defined in at least one dictionary as "such as to excite contempt by smallness, poor quality etc."

Your comments were captured and highlighted by the print and broadcast media on a broad scale in Montreal both on Thursday the 29th and Friday the 30th and judging from the reactions expressed at that time your statement certainly was successful at eliciting contempt from the Montreal community regarding the competency of our employees who are currently engaged in marketing and sales efforts.

We believe that disparaging statements of this type from members of the ownership group are unjustified, irresponsible and disrespectful of many of our employees who have the ungrateful task of generating attendance and sponsorships during these difficult times. Your comments also indicate a profound lack of understanding of the realities of professional sports marketing. To some extent your comments also call into question the business sense of those sponsors and the loyalty of the fans who, notwithstanding the current turmoil, have committed to the Club. After all, who wants to associate publicly with people who have been characterized as pitiful.

The reality of the current situation is that all of the employees involved in marketing and sales have for many months had to deal with strong client and fan resistance regarding the Expos' product for this season. The uncertainty regarding the Club's continued presence in Montreal is the main stumbling block to generating business. Resolving this problem is more dependent on your efforts than it is on the efforts of the Expo's employees. They should not have to pay for the conflict between you and Claude Brochu.

Notwithstanding the significant challenge that selling the Expos represents, our marketing and sales employees have remained loyal and hard working. We wish to remind you that many of these employees are young with families to support. They are often involved in double shift days with sales and marketing work during the day and client service during the games.
... 2

These employees have carried on their work even in the knowledge that their jobs may shortly be ended. They are very concerned about their ability to find meaningful employment elsewhere if they are branded publicly as being associated with a group that does pitiful work.

We were surprised to hear such comments coming the President of the Fonds de solidarité de la FTQ, who is supposed to defend workers, not undermine their credibility.

Your comments have had a demoralizing impact on every employee, as all the departments were involved in putting together the McGwire promotion. We respectfully request that you refrain from future statements of this type regarding marketing and sales or any other department.

Thank you for your co-operation and understanding.

Sincerely,

Laurier M. Carpentier
Executive Vice-President, Development

Richard Morency
Vice-President, Sales & Marketing

Claude Delorme
Vice-President, Stadium Operations

Johanne Héroux
Vice-President, Communications

Michel Bussière
Vice-President, Finance & Treasurer

<u>CONFIDENTIAL</u>

May 3, 1999

Mr. Jacques Menard
Nesbitt Burns Inc.
Suite 3200
1501 McGill College
Montreal, Quebec
H3A 3M8

Dear Jacques,

All of us whose lives and livelihoods revolve around the Expos continue to operate as best we can in the face of the uncertainty of the future of baseball in Montreal, coupled with the battle between Claude Brochu and some of his dissident partners, including yourself, which continues to be played so emotionally in the media. Like Felipe Alou, his coaches and our twenty-five players, those of us who are Expos employees consider ourselves a team. While we are not always right, we always work hard to be right. While we do not always agree with one another, we do work together to achieve the best results we can for the team.

This is a letter I probably should have written toward the end of last year, when, to the delight of the media, you and some of your partners were fueling the emotional Brochu bashing that continues to this day. But Claude Bachand's recent public criticism of our marketing efforts in preparation for the St. Louis series was the last straw for me.

Without going into the merits of Mr. Bachand's comments, I would like someone with any amount of business sense to tell me what possible good can result when an owner (or someone representing an owner) of a company makes public comments that degrade the company's own employees. Many of us who work for the Expos not only disagree with Mr. Bachand, but we resent his taking destructive public shots at our team.

Claude Bachand's haven't been the only harmful comments from members of your group. Jocelyn Proteau, Mark Routtenberg, Pierre Michaud, Paul Roberge, Jean Coutu and you have all taken turns at inciting the media to join you in a public relations campaign reminiscent of some of the dirtiest political campaigns in memory, mostly directed at Claude Brochu. Who in your group thinks that such public relations efforts will help achieve a long-term solution to keep baseball in Montreal? Has this caused anyone inside or outside your group to focus on the real challenges to achieve this result, or rather are you more intent on deflecting public attention from the real issues? To their credit, those who represent Canadian Pacific, BCE, Telemedia, McClelland and Stewart, and Cascades Inc. appear to have steered clear of your smear campaign.

My own view is that you and some of your group are more concerned with finding someone to blame for your possible failure than you are with focusing on the issues that will save baseball for Montreal. I am therefore concerned that you are particularly focused on setting the groundwork for the departure of baseball from Montreal.

. . . /2

If you fail to keep the club in Montreal, will you try to pin it on Claude Brochu? The Expos marketing department? Bud Selig? Some imagined conspiracy within Major League Baseball? Or rather will it be that you couldn't muster the necessary government, corporate and public interest, assemble sufficient investor capital, build a suitable stadium or come up with a reasonable business plan to ensure the long-term health of the baseball business in Montreal?

Expos employees want neither of the above. We prefer that you to find a long-term solution to keep the club in Montreal and to put us in a financial position where we can compete on the field.

In the interim, however, I suggest that you and your prospective partners stop this silly finger-pointing campaign, as it is doing nothing to advance your chance for success, while it is very harmful to the morale of Expos employees. Keep in mind that when you take shots at Claude Brochu, Richard Morency, our marketing employees, or anyone else working for this team, you are shooting at my teammates. I hope you will understand when I say I resent it. More importantly, I hope you understand that such emotional nonsense is not productive.

Yours truly,

Bill Stoneman
Vice-President, Baseball Operations

260

Office of the Commissioner
MAJOR LEAGUE BASEBALL

June 28, 1999

ROBERT A. DuPUY
Executive Vice President
Administration and Chief Legal Officer

Via Facsimile - 514/286-7287

Mr. L. Jacques Menard
c/o Nesbitt Burns
1501 McGill College Ave.
Suite 3200
Montreal, Quebec H3A 3M8

Dear Jacques:

Paul, Len and I appreciate having had the opportunity to meet with you on June 17. While it is disappointing that we have not brought any of the various open items to conclusion, the meeting provided an opportunity for a substantive update and a full exchange on the issues surrounding your new stadium construction and business plan.

Through our various exchanges of correspondence and meetings over the past nine months, certain axioms have emerged:

1. The Montreal Expos cannot compete economically without a new stadium and a stadium which serves as a destination point and not just a facility to conduct games.

2. Everyone seems to agree to open the stadium by opening day, 2002, that construction must begin not later than January 1, 2000.

3. Major League Baseball cannot countenance the continuation of the current situation. The Commissioner views it as imperative that the long-term future of the Expos' franchise be determined now to allow plans for 2000, including the schedule, to be finalized.

4. There were and remain a number of complex and unresolved government and financial issues. While some progress has been made and while your efforts have been diligent, we need to reach closure.

With that in mind, the Commissioner believes it critical in light of the various discussions to establish a fair but tight timeline to come to closure. The time has come for final decision-making and those decisions should be made with as much information and as many established conclusions as possible.

245 Park Avenue, New York, NY 10167 (212) 931-7800 http://www.majorleaguebaseball.com

261

1. By July 15 – consistent with your assertions – complete negotiations for the acquisition of the land, and document the structure and annual cost.

2. By July 15, provide written confirmation from the appropriate governmental entity or a written legal opinion letter, that the property tax exemption will continue in a new park and would survive a legal challenge.

3. We recognize that the zoning approvals cannot be accomplished in the next 30 days. However, by July 15, please provide in writing each step in the timeline for obtaining approval, the possible issues, if any, in each step, what has to be done in preparation for each step, and your best (and reasonable) view of when each step will be completed.

4. Per your own assertions, we understand you intend to select one design firm by the end of this month. By July 23, we would like a reconciliation, in writing, of the issues raised by HOK and Arthur Andersen based on your most current information and design drawing. We still have serious concerns not only about the estimated cost of the stadium, but also about the nature (and, therefore, desirability) of the facility currently proposed. We also remain concerned about the design and build process, and the owners' continuing ability to control the construction. We need as much information as possible to allow the Commissioner and Ownership Committee to continue their deliberations and make decisions in a timely manner. Any confirmed agreement with respect to changes in design or cost should also be provided.

5. Obviously, your acknowledgement that the PSL program will not yield the original economic projections is troubling. Based on your numbers, this creates a new shortfall of $50 million. As you know, we have been concerned about these projections from the inception of our discussions. By July 15, please provide in writing your plan for dealing with that shortfall. Your response to the next item may well encompass this point.

6. By July 15, we would like in writing your most current financial projections. By July 23 we would like in writing letters of intent from each of your committed proposed and continuing investors to that point in the amounts they intend to invest. Given the issues about construction costs, and given the concerns about the PSL program, we also believe it is critical to include an acknowledgment of the right of the control person to make mandatory cash calls. This is consistent with what was done (and utilized) in Arizona and other locations. Also, given your current business plans, please have your investors include an acknowledgement that there is no assurance of continuing revenue sharing and losses may well have to be funded from such calls.

7. By July 23, the completion and signing of your loan/grant documents with the Provincial Government. We have a draft of those documents. Jeff White will provide his comments promptly. You have indicated some open issues with respect to repayment schedule, etc., which we assume will be resolved by that date.

8. By July 8, a written acknowledgement that you have completed your agreement with Claude Brochu if Baseball agrees to your going forward in Montreal. We understand you have already reached an agreement in principle.

9. By July 23, a written acknowledgement that you have resolved all governance and partnership tax issues.

We recognize that this is an ambitious schedule. Our objective, as mentioned above, is to make Baseball's decisions in the best-informed environment possible. We believe we have included only those items we deem critical. We remain open to continuing our dialogue and moving the process forward.

Thank you for your continuing efforts.

Very truly yours,

Robert A. DuPuy

cc: Commissioner Allan H. Selig
Claude Brochu
Paul Beeston
Leonard S. Coleman, Jr.
Thomas J. Ostertag
Robert J. Kheel